Life with God

The Unusual Adventure

Susan Abraham

Gotham Books
30 N Gould St.
Ste. 20820, Sheridan, WY 82801
https://gothambooksinc.com/

Phone: 1 (307) 464-7800

© 2023 *Susan Abraham*. All rights reserved.

No part of this book may be reproduced, stored in a retrieval system, or transmitted by any means without the written permission of the author.

Published by Gotham Books (January 31, 2023)

ISBN: 979-8-88775-211-2 (H)
ISBN: 979-8-88775-209-9 (P)
ISBN: 979-8-88775-210-5 (E)

Because of the dynamic nature of the Internet, any web addresses or links contained in this book may have changed since publication and may no longer be valid.

The views expressed in this work are solely those of the author and do not necessarily reflect the views of the publisher, and the publisher hereby disclaims any responsibility for them.

Acknowledgement

My greatest acknowledgement goes to the Almighty God. He has watched over my life from conception and birth to this stage in my life and I believe He will continue until I meet with Him after this life. He has made me who I am. His hand of blessing has been on my life in a way that I sometimes marvel. He is my Father. All that I have is from Him. As long as I live, I will live for Him, and in death, I will be with Him in glory. He is my life!

My next acknowledgement goes to my husband who has helped me to grow and mature in relating with him. His birthday present on my 48th birthday inspired this writing.

My children are my jewels. They made me a mum and helped me grow up in the process. They also helped me recapture my childhood. I acknowledge and love them very much.

Contents

Introduction

Phase 1

Birth & Childhood .... Chapter 1

Teenage Years and Early Adulthood .... Chapter 2

Awareness of True and False Spirituality .... Chapter 3

The Born-Again Experience and Life .... Chapter 4

Phase 2

Marriage .... Chapter 5

Relocating Abroad and Starting the Family .... Chapter 6

Moving to West .... Chapter 7

Navigating Cultures .... Chapter 8

Phase 3

Work Experiences .... Chapter 9

Spiritual Experiences .... Chapter 10

Church Experiences .... Chapter 11

Conclusion

Notes / Reflection

Introduction

There is always joy when a baby is born into the family unless in unusual situations. But who can tell the future of a new born baby? The pathway of every life is unprecedented. Born in a remote village in Africa, a baby girl grew spiritually, physically, emotionally, mentally and socially strong through all the adversities that surrounded her, in her family and in her community. Her teenage years were full of instability, yet she thrived and grew into a young adult with determination and purpose. At that stage she had an encounter with her creator that transformed her life and propelled her to live differently.

This is Lily's life story. You may experience a barrage of emotions as you read, some comfortable and some uncomfortable. My hope as the writer is that you will be encouraged, inspired, challenged, motivated and blessed from this story. God is real, alive and is working in us, for us and through us! Most times we are not aware of His Presence. It is a double blessing when we become aware of Him and co-operate with Him. This is when we can have endless adventures in this reality called Life.

Chapter 1

Birth & Childhood

God is the creator of Life:

'You made all the delicate, inner parts of my body and knit me together in my mother's womb. Thank you for making me so wonderfully complex! Your workmanship is marvelous how well I know. You watched me as I was being formed in utter seclusion, as I was woven together in the dark of the womb. You saw me before I was born. Every day of my life was recorded in your book. Every moment was laid out before a single day had passed' (Psalm 139:13-18 NLT).

In the tropical suburb, surrounded by tall palms, fruit trees, shrubs and all kinds of vegetation, a young mother gave birth to her fifth child, behold, it was a girl. She named her Lily. Her first four children; Noah, Prosper, David and Elijah (three boys and one girl) were excited to have another sibling. They loved helping mother to look after this new arrival. She was surrounded with love. Her father had three other wives and seventeen children. All these wives and children lived with him in one large compound prior to a civil the war. Lily's mother was his second wife, and his relationship with her was flout with instability, repeated separation and reunion. Lily's birth came after their recent reunion from many years of separation. It was indeed an unusual relationship, not the norm in those days. Their love story was certainly unique because a year after, Lily's mother gave birth to her sixth baby, a boy. She named him Daniel.

About some weeks after the birth of Daniel, a civil war broke out in their country. This war shattered the unity, peace and serenity in Lily's family. Prior to the war, they all live together in a huge compound and went to one church, her father's church that was in the compound. The church was a Spiritual Church. Its headquarters was in another town about 500 miles away. Her father wanted to evacuate his whole family to this headquarters but her mother refused to go. According to her mother, she refused to go there because she sensed the spirituality in this church was not right. So her husband decided to take her two older children, Prosper and David, his first wife and the rest of his children and fled to this place, leaving Lily's mother with a new born baby; Daniel, a toddler; Lily and her immediate older brother, Elijah who was 3 years old. His remaining two wives had to make their individual choices because they did not want to go with him. One went back to her family homes with her children, the other got married to another man.

As the war intensified and the frontline moved closer to their village, Lily's mother fled to her family with her three youngest children and older son, Noah, who refused to go with his father because he wanted to stay and help his mother with the babies. Unfortunately, Lily's mother had a difficult time with her step-brothers in her family as both of her parents were dead; her only sister was married and away. These step-brothers did not welcome her and her children well into the family. She gathered her flock, moved to and stayed with distant relatives who were kind enough to provide them with logging, provision and care until the war was over. On top of suffering from the trauma of the war, Lily's mother also lost her baby, Daniel who died due to malnutrition. It is hard to imagine the grief, struggle and stress they all went through. The ravages of war are devastating to individuals and families. The loss and subsequent effect of the trauma of wars can be irreversible. In Lily's young mind was full of confusion, grief, fears and terror. The impact of this trauma was long lasting in Lily's family and subsequent generations. Life never returned to normal thereafter.

After the war, Lily's mother brought her remaining children back home only to encounter another problem. Her husband will not accept her into the family home. The reason was based on his spiritual belief. As twisted as this sounds, to him it was true; he believed his wife and children were defiled during the separation. So he told Lily's mother to go to the headquarters of his church with her children for the cleansing rituals. Lily's mother was a stubborn woman. She refused and decided to go and live in one of the vacant buildings in the community with her children. Life was not easy as she needed to fend for her family without any support. But she was a strong and very industrious woman. She somehow found a way to do some mini business ventures that helped her to provide her children with daily meals and clothing. The downside of that was that her children, age between 7 and 5 also had to grow faster than their age and be able to take care of themselves as they were on their own most hours of the day. Amazing, they did. An evidence that physical difficulty cannot break a person but rather make them strong, innovative and even more creative. Her older son, Noah went away during this season to fend for himself. He was a teenager now but assumed the role of a man. He will visit mother regularly with presents for her and his siblings.

A unique thing happened during this time: The man who had the vacant house they lived in came back after the war ended as well. He got into a relationship with Lily's mother. This resulted in the birth of a baby girl. Mother called her Grace. Just before Grace's birth, this man who impregnated Lily's mother had kicked her and her out of his house. She was in the last trimester of the pregnancy then. How awful! Another family took them in. They were grateful for this great help. Grace was born during a church conference, a happy and joyous time. This is the church Lily's mother attended with her children. The pastor and wife took care of them, feeding and clothing them. They kept her mother and the baby with them till she was strong enough to return home, about two miles away. Noah came home one day with the baby's needs; bath, nappies and cloths and other presents for the family. Neighbours rally around to supply them with meals every day. Lily was happy to welcome her baby sister. She became very fun of Grace and developed some strong attachment to her. So much such that she became the baby sitter for her mother who still had to work hard to fend for them. Lily was six years old when Grace was born.

A year before, at the age of five, Lily had started Primary School. Lily was fascinated and excited about school even from a younger age. The usual age for starting Primary school then was at six years. Mother had to enroll her early because she used to follow her immediate older brother, Elijah to school every day. She would run after him, cry and refused to be comforted if not allowed to follow him. Even when the teacher would not let her into his class, Lily would hang around at the door and waited till the day was over and then went home with her brother. When Elijah's teacher eventually accepted Lily into the class, she realized Lily was able to listen, eager to learn and even better than some of those of school age. The School was two miles away from their home. So at this tender age, Lily used to walk four miles daily to and from School. To her, this was not a problem. School was the most exciting and happy place to be. She loved learning new things every day. Some mornings, there was no breakfast. Lily's mother would tell her not to go to school. She was worried Lily would not survive the long walk with hunger. But Lily would cry till she let her go. You wonder how she survived the long journey to and from school with an empty stomach. Some days when mother has some money, she will give Lily a penny for bean's cake for lunch. She was a loving and caring mother. But Lily had developed such sympathy for her mother and wouldn't spend this money.

She saved this pennies and gave them back to her on the weekend. Mother was amazed and wonder how she survived daily in school.

However, she was not worried because Lily was always happy to go to School. All Lily knew was that going to School was her passion, her highlight and her happy place. Lily had good teachers as well who loved and encouraged her. They used to mark her writing board after every work with a very big right tick. Lily was happy and very proud of this and eager to show this to her mother at the end of the day. Her mother's praise was also additional encouragement and her source of resilience.

The first three years in Primary School was free, school fees was applicable from year four. This marked a turning point in Lily's life. He mother could not pay these fees. At the end of that year three, mother sat Lily down and explained her predicament. She however, reassured Lily that her father would pay the fees for her but only with a condition that Lily lives with him. Lily loves living with her mother and siblings in this one room given to them by a neighbour. She used to visit her father who lived in a brick house, in his big compound with her step brothers and sisters, and no wife. He was always nice to Lily though. Whenever she visited him, he will give her the favourite food that she loves; a bunch of green bananas. He had many banana trees in his compound, and told Lily whenever she visited how he preserved the best for her. He then harvested it and make one of Lily's step brother to carry it for her and back to her mother. So Lily thought the deal to go and live with him was not that bad. She was quite happy to accept it so she can continue to go to School and besides her mother's house was on her way to School. She figured out she would still be able to visit her mother and siblings. Deal was sealed, before the start of the next term Lily moved into her father's compound.

However, things did not turn out as planned. Lily did continue in school with her father's help in paying the school fees but within that term, one of Lily's step sister who was married and had a young family came home. She made a request to her father to take Lily away with her as a baby sitter. She assured him that she would definitely allow Lily to continue in School by paying the fees. Her father relayed the information to Lily and asked if she would like to go with them. Lily's only condition of going to School being promised, she had no reason to object. She gave her consent and went with them. Her step-sister's husband was in the military, so they move around a lot and often. This season, there were in a town, about 203.8km or 126.6miles from their home town. They had two children, a girl and a boy. The girl was about two years old and the boy was just a baby. Lily clicked with the children, loved them and loved to take care of them. The baby got even more attached to Lily than to the mother. How can that be? You may ask. Read on and you will find out.

Lily's transition to this family was during the first term holiday of her year four in Primary School. When the next term was about to start, Lily overheard a conversation between her step-sister and her husband in their bedroom. The husband asked, 'When will you go shopping for your sister's uniform so she can start School?' Her step-sister responded, 'Who said I brought her here for School? All I wanted was for her to come and babysit for me'. Lily was surprised but could not believe her ears. She could not imagine why this step-sister would be that mean to her. However, the confirmation of her aim began to manifest when the School actually started. She had no intention of letting Lily go to School. Lily was unhappy and grieved. Every day, she stood by the balcony and watched with longing in her heart at other children in lovely uniforms going to School and cried. After a while, she could take it no more! She became angry and started to be naughty to her step-sister.

Lily still loved and took care of the children but she refused to do the housework. In anger, she even destroyed some of her step-sister's ceramic housewares. Off course, her step-sister was not happy. She started to talk to Lily in threatening ways but to her surprise, Lily answered her back. This was not expected in this culture; children were to be seen and not heard no matter what they went through. Lily was not accepting this injustice and eventually ran away from the house one day and wondered in the town from morning till dusk. Lily was only nine years old then. She wanted to go back to her father but she did not know the way. Her step-sister's husband who was at work came home at the end of the day and looked for Lily. He eventually found her sleeping in one of the public park benches in the night, and took her back to the house. Lily wept and struggled with him all the way back and told him she wanted to go back to her parents. He was a nice man. He pleaded with Lily and promised he would arrange that. When they came back to the house, the baby boy has been crying almost throughout the day. He missed Lily so much and refused to be comforted by his mother. When Lily picked him up, he released streams of shallow breath clinging to her. He was hungry and exhausted. Lily hugged, washed and fed him. He slept in her arms before she put him into his cot. That is how attached the baby had become to Lily. The mother did have a difficult day in Lily's absence. On Lily's part, from then on, she showed her step sister in every attitude, word and action that she does not want to live with them anymore. She has had enough of her step-sister's deception, manipulation and control.

Finally, the day came this step sister could not tolerate Lily anymore and she decided to take Lily back home to their father. Between her and father, she told him all of Lily's naughty ways, attitude and actions, confirming that was the reason she brought Lily back home. Their father was surprised that Lily could behave that way. He called Lily into her presence and asked why she behaved that badly with her step-sister.

Lily simply responded, 'Because she did not let me go to school'. Their father was very angry when he heard this and cursed the step-sister for deceiving him. A few days later, this step-sister developed a mental health problem. Sadly she never recovered from this. She died with it many years later. Their father explained that god was punishing her because of her sins. Lily had a faint idea that the god her father worship is a very angry and ruthless god. She also thought her step-sister deserved this punishment for depriving her of education, the only thing she loved in life in such a devious way.

Lily really missed her mother when she came back home. She could not even visit her because she was no longer living where she was. Her father explained her mother had finally accepted to go to the headquarters of his church for the purification rituals. This was about 86.2 km away from their town. Lily could not just go there because she wanted to. What really happened was that Lily's senior sister, Prosper, who was also married, was about to give birth to her first child. Tradition had it that the mother must take care of her for a while after this first delivery. Lily's father used that opportunity to manipulate and control her mother. He made it a condition that for him to allow Prosper to be cared for by her mother, mother has to go to this place. Lily's mother had no choice but to accept the condition. That's how powerless and helpless women were in those days in this community.

Lily also missed attending to the church her mother used to take her and her siblings to. She had loved everything about this church and was very active in it even at a young age. She loved the singing, the hand clapping and dancing, and she was in the children's choir. Lily had lost so much within this time that her life was not a happy one. She was depressed, frustrated and angry. She began to bully her step-sister's daughter at some point. She did not like her father's church either and hated to be woken up at 05:00 for prayers by her father. This was part of her father's rituals and he always made sure his children took part in it. Sometimes he would pour cold water on the children just to wake them up. There was nothing nice about this at all, it actually felt cruel.

The only thing that brought some comfort into Lily's heart was re-starting

Primary School. Her father was quick to re-instate that for her. Unfortunately, the following year her father died. Lily was only ten years old. Lily's young mind did not understand bereavement. She could not even weep at the funeral. The only impact his dead would have had on her would have been the interruption in her education.

However, God made a way for her to continue in School. He raised up her second brother, David to become her new father, her daddy. David had just finished from Secondary school and had a job with a company. After the burial, he took Lily away. Lily lived with him and he was just delighted to see to it that she went to School. He supported her through the rest of her Primary School years, Secondary School, through higher education, and till she got employed, received her first proper salary and began to live independently. David's sacrificial love, care, provision, guidance and discipline were all that Lily needed in a father to direct her young life. She began to live well and flourish under his supervision.

Lily's Mother

Lily's mother was a remarkable woman; she was about four feet tall, strong, full of energy, industrious and very hard working. She was from a different town with a different culture and ways of life. That was where they stayed during the war. Her ways, attitudes and actions were not like other women in her days either. She was quite outrageous, fearless, loved her children more than her life. She was so petite but larger than life in her words, attitudes and actions. Every day, she woke up before dawn, walked for about three miles to one of the big markets in town. There she bought some food in bulk and bring them back to their local market where she sold to final consumers. That was her business. And through this she generated enough income to feed and clothe her three young children; Elijah (9), Lily (6) and Grace (the baby). Even when she was pregnant with Grace, she never stopped. She has been working this way even when Elijah and Lily were younger, leaving them on their own all day. At 4 years of age, Lily was able to take mother's instructions on what to do and eat the next day when she would not be there. Elijah was somehow naughty and mother could not rely on him much though he was older, to carry out her instructions but on Lily. After witnessing mother beating up Elijah for his repeated naughtiness many times, Lily became an adaptable child, and so avoided mother's fiery temper. When mother became stronger after Grace's birth and able to resume her trading, she used to carry the baby on her back to all these markets. Lily would baby sit when she was back or on Sundays. Lily's mother had a fiery temper. However, behind that fiery anger was a woman who loved her children and was willing to sacrifice her life for them. If anyone hurts any of her children, mother went after them with such anger that they never dared next time. In Lily's later years, she used to be embarrassed by her anger, so she won't tell mother if someone has bullied her. However, she learned to stand up for herself. Mother was always very proud of Lily's success with school work. Lily was a brilliant little girl; she always come first in the exams and had good reports from her teachers in terms of behaviour and attitudes to school work. Mother always sang and danced at the news of this success while all their neighbours watch. Lily used to feel embarrassed and would run and hide.

Mother's marriage to Lily's father was not a happy one. Lily did not understand at this tender age why they live in different houses in the same community. Once, Lily witnessed her father came into the house they lived wielding a machete, attacking her mother and accusing her for stealing his palm fruit. Her mother was crying and pleading with him. Lily was scared, she held tight to her mother's leg and cried till her father left. Mother hugged and comforted her thereafter. Later in her life, she used to question mother why she choose to stay with her father despite his abusive ways towards her. Lily did not know the trauma she witnessed has caused fear to develop in her heart towards her father. This became a spontaneous reaction later in her life towards male authority figures.

Her mother's response to her question was, 'Because of you my children'. Lily did not understand her then but did after having her own children. A mother's love for her children overrides her love for every other thing, even her life, comfort and pleasures.

Lily's mother was a believer; she had knowledge of the True God. The best legacy she left in Lily's life. She was a member of The Apostolic Church, and used to take her children to every Sunday service and other activities in the church. Lily grew up to love going to this church Sunday Schools and sang in the children's choir from a very early age. Lily loves to sing! She had great fun taking part in these activities though she did not really have a personal relationship with God. Her mother used to tell them the god her father has is not good. That was the reason for some of the conflict in their relationship but she refused to leave him and marry another man because of her children. Though Lily did not fully understand this, mother's words were enough to keep her vigilant whenever she attended any church. At some point in her life, she chose to attend only The Apostolic Church wherever she attended, knowing this God is good and would look after her. And she did experienced His goodness. You will hear more about this later in this book. Reconciling and compromising to her husband was the most tragic thing in Lily's mother's life. Subsequently, her mental illness one year after his death was the greatest trauma Lily ever suffered in this life. The lesson Lily learned from her mother's life later is that believing in God is not enough.

She needed to know the truth in God's words, the Bible, and live by this truth. Sometimes, Lily felt if her mother had known the truth in God's word and stayed with it, refused to compromise with her father, she might have been able to pray her whole family into salvation.

Lily's mother never recovered completely from the mental illness. She lived in her husband's compound later in life, and was cared for by her sons; David and Elijah and their families till she died at the age of 80 years. Lily was abroad at this time but she did question the Lord. The Lord comforted her. He showed Lily in a dream how he rescued her mother and took her home with him.

Lily's Father

Lily's father on the other hand was a tall man, about 6 feet plus. He was considered one of the richest men in the village. He had lots of lands and palm fruit trees; a symbol of wealth in those days. He was also an educated man; he worked in the Hospitals as a Pharmacy Technician before the war. He retired thereafter as he was not working when Lily got to know him. Most villagers used to call him doctor. When Lily got to know him after the war, he lived in a big compound and in a brick house with his children from his different wives, including Lily's older sister, Prosper, and second brother, David. Before, Lily used to visit him before the time she finally moved in to live with him because of the school fees issue. He was a good man. He used to be nice to Lily and would give her whatever she asked of him. He had lots of fruit trees in his compound; these were pears, mangoes, apple, banana, plantain and grapefruit. Lily loved climbing the apple tree, sat there and ate some juicy apples. At the end of the visit, she usually chose one of these bunches of bananas and asked father for it. He at times would even show her a bigger bunch he had reserved for her. He then harvested it and made one of Lily's step-brother who was stronger to carry it and escort her home to her mother.

Lily's father was also a farmer; he had large farms with yams, cassava, many vegetables and other root crops. All of his children used to help with the farm works and enjoyed the harvest, especially the yam harvest which was a very special one. He gave each of the children their own yams at the end of the harvest. Once he gave Lily a lovely size yam when she was living with him. One of Lily's step-sibling stole her yam because they were jealous of her. She remembered going to where she kept her yam only to find it missing. She was sad and cried for it. Her father, whose room was next to theirs, came out to ask what the matter was. She told him and he only responded with, 'Don't worry, I will give you a bigger one'. Then he left and went back to his room. Lily kept crying because she was not comforted. The next thing she knew, her father came in and just gave her a whipped on her back. This shocked and silenced her. She had never experienced his anger till then. He later told her he was trying to rest after all the hard work of harvest but her cry was disturbing him. He did keep his promise after all; he gave her a bigger yam, and that made her happy.

Apart from the vegetable farming, Lily's father also reared some animals; goats, sheep and chickens. Some of these were used for foods as well. He was mostly self-sufficient. His choice to live only with the children was because he wanted to have peace from the conflict that his many wives were creating. But this left someone wondering about that because there was always conflict with the children. Maybe to him, handling children's conflict was easier than dealing with that of the wives. Lily always remembered being bullied by her older step-sister. This stepsister was the oldest and in charge of the household at that time. Her brother was older than Lily but Lily was stronger physically and mentally than him. So this step-sister, because she was in charge of the house used to give Lily more work to do and less food when it came to food allocation. One day, Lily had enough. She refused to do the work and told her to be fair by giving her brother the bigger portion of the work as he had the bigger portion of food. This was some weeding work in the farm. This step-sister refused to play fair. Lily left the work and went and reported it to their father. He listened and gave Lily justice; gave her more food to satisfy her hunger, and then told her to go and rest in his room. He made this step-sister to do Lily's share of the work. She was not happy with Lily at all and persecuted her in discreet ways. It was good when Lily used to visit them because she was able to run back to her mother for refuge when situations got too nasty but living permanently with them was not nice. The good thing was that that season was short for Lily.

Lily's Father had his own church in his compound, it was a Spiritual Church and in a separate building. Mother used to tell her the story of how her father got into this Spiritual Church. Her father used to go to the Methodist Church when they were married. This Spiritual Church was the main cause of the conflict between them. Lily never grew up to know any of her grand-parents, uncles and aunties on her father's side. They all died young with one strange illness or another. Mother said, her father had a friend who was attending this Spiritual Church. This friend one day visited father and told him about his church. He said if father joined him in that church, he would not die young as the rest of his siblings. Lily's father decided to test it out. He used to go intermittently until his retirement. He became more serious with the church after his retirement. By this time, he has tasted the power in this church and swallowed the bait. Unfortunately, he did not know he has been deceived; this power was not from the true God but from the devil that came to steal, kill and destroy.

And that's exactly what the devil did to him and then to his family; first he stole his heart by displaying some fake healing powers, then killed and destroyed him. Lily's father was very sincere and devoted in worshipping what he did not know. The most terrible deception. His belief was based on the Old Testament scriptures. He practiced all the sacrifices there and made his family do it as well. He used to wake the children up as early as 05:00 every morning for prayers and would read the Psalms to them. At her young age, Lily never knew the difference but her mother knew, and she believed by staying around, not marrying another man, she could protect her children. Somehow, she was right except she was not wise enough as she ended up being drawn into it through compromise. It is very sad father was so deceived; he could read the

Bible because he was educated but he never read beyond the Old Testament. He could have come to 1 Corinthians 10:20 which says;

'But I say, that the things which the Gentiles sacrifice, they sacrifice to devils, and not to God: and I would not that you have fellowship with devils'

Probably his eyes of understanding would have been opened if he had read the above and he would have understood how Jesus became his sacrifice for sin. And he did not have to do those rituals which opened his life and family to the devil and his demonic invasion. He and is household could have been saved if he had known and accepted the truth in the scriptures.

Lily's mother on the other hand was illiterate; she could not read for herself and did not understand God's words or the power in it. When Lily later on challenged her for her decision to compromise and eventually went to live in the headquarters of her father's church, this was when Lily became a born-again believer, she used to tell Lily, 'I did not believe in their god. I still used to go out to The Apostolic Church'. But she did not know the word in 2 Corinthians 6:17;

'Wherefore come out from among them, and be ye separate, saith the Lord, and touch not the unclean thing; and I will receive you'.

The devil is too crafty for anyone to mess with. If he cannot kill you, he will draw you in. Lily's mother used to warn her children; do not go to any of their feast, celebration and sacrifices but you cannot live among them and be safe. The wisest thing to do is to come out from among them.

Lily learned a lot from her parent's mistakes.

Lily at the age of 50 plus, still remembers the day her father died very vividly; it was the 10th of February 1976. Prior to this, he did not plant his

yams as usual which was always in January of every year. Lily remember walking around with him in the farm and asking him why. His response was, 'If only those in the heavens will allow me'. Lily used to wonder why God did not allow you to cultivate your land but he never explained more than that to her inquisitive young mind.

Then on this eventful day, Lily had served him his tapioca, prepared the way he likes it which was on the previous day. Among all of his children, he used to like Lily's way of preparing this the most. And Lily loved to see him proud of her. So she made sure she served him before leaving for school. Lily was in Primary four and 10 years old. When she took the food to her father's room, he just asked her to put it on the table saying he would eat it later. Lily felt something was not right as he never behaved that way before. But they, the children left for school anyway. When they came back, their father was still in bed and shivering with fever. He had sent for their oldest step-sister, and that one was in the room with him. The children were told not to disturb him because he was not well, and they had to carry on with their normal after school duties.

One was going into the bush to fetch some grass for the goats.

Lily remembered thinking while doing this that her father may die. She did not know where this thought came from. All she knew was that she has never seen her father ill, so this illness was very unusual. Father did not want to be taken to the hospital. Rather, he sent for one of the elders in his church to come and do some sacrifices for him believing he is atoning for his sins and clearing his way for a better after-life. How absurd; the devil is wicked. That night, he asked two of his older sons to sleep in his room. They were the ones who witness his death around midnight. They came out of the room screaming, the children all woke up and rushed to his room. In Lily's young mind, he was lying like he was sleeping. She did not understand why others were crying because she could not. She thought he was only sleeping. Lily's older step-siblings rushed around informing his friends, his church, his first wife and her mother who came back from the headquarters of his church. By the evening of the next day, he was buried in his room. This was when fear gripped young Lily's heart. It was hard to accept her father's body was under the ground in his room and she could bump into him as a ghost when she entered this room. Lily dreaded going into his room unless there were other people there. She did overcome this fear later in life and even slept alone in this room. There was no ghost either to scare her.

Nevertheless, Lily still feels sad and angry whenever she thinks of her father. He devoted his life worshipping what he did not know, and died in the deception. And subsequently, his family has experienced tremendous affliction, suffering and loss as a result of his mistake, even after his death. The worst thing to happen to any human being is believing a lie from the devil, and dying in that state. This became part of Lily's resolve and motivation to help people know the truth, so they can be free from deception from the devil and his demons. Satan is very wicked and hates human beings. Humans need to be aware of him, his deceptive, manipulative and controlling ways.

Lily's mother and step-mother returned to where they were residing after Lily's father's burial. Lily's mother had engaged herself in her usual business there. The market that she got her wholesale products from which were mostly shell fish was about 10 miles away from their residence, and by the sea side. Lily once went with her when she visited her. She requested to go to this market, eager to help mother. However, mother tried to discourage her but Lily held on persuading mother. One day, mother eventually let her. Lily was crying on her way back because she was so tired and there was no public transport on the way. Mother just kept reminding her that it was her choice. Lily managed to get home that day and never had the desire to follow her anymore.

The family home was still occupied by some of Lily's step-siblings after her father's death and burial. Father's church sent one of their priests to live in the compound and carry out their rituals. His sustenance was probably not possible because the situation had changed. Lily was living with David then. One day, Lily's mother sent someone to David with a complaint. Apparently, she was told David wanted her at home. She came and waited there for him but it turned out he never made this request of her. It was all a manipulation. During her stay at home, and at one of the times the rest of the children still gathered with this priest, a prophecy came through one of the children, telling Lily's mother she has been chosen to come back home and serve in the church. You see, the devil can also prophesy. Lily's mother was actually angry with David thinking he was the reason why she came home to experience that nonsense (that was how she saw it without knowing she has been trapped). After David clarified the issue, she went back ignoring the whole incident.

At the same time, Lily's mother reported her older son, Noah being taken by his step-mother, father's first wife into a meeting with the elders of the church. She told him it was time for him to receive the inheritance his father left for him. Noah went and after reported to his mother the rituals he was made to undergo. The following year, Noah returned to the family home to carry on with his inheritance. Sad to say his mind and subsequently life has remained unproductive, he became mentally ill. Lily's mother developed mental illness as well and was returned to the family home. Lily became an orphan but the Lord picked her up and cared for her.

Conclusion

In concluding this chapter, the encouragement to the reader is to trust in God, the True God and Jesus Christ, His Son. He sure has a plan for you. He is faithful and passionate to see to it that this plan is fulfilled in your life according to His words;

'For I know the plans I have for you,' says the Lord. 'They are plans for good and not for disaster, to give you a future and a hope' (Jeremiah 29:11) NLT

Hold on to that dream in your heart, pursue and don not let go. He will surely make a way for you.

Some people are so broken and do not even have a dream. He can heal you in every way you hurt, restore your soul and help you dream again.

In John 10:10 - 11, Jesus said,

'…My purpose is to give them a rich and satisfying life. I am the good shepherd. The good shepherd sacrifices his life for the sheep'. (NLT)

You can stand on Psalm 23.

The Passion Translation puts it this way:

'The Lord is my best friend and my shepherd; I always have more than enough. He offers a resting place for me in his luxurious love. His tracks take me to an oasis of peace, the quiet brook of bliss. That's where he restores and revives my life. He opens before me pathways to God's pleasure and leads me along in his footsteps of righteousness so that I can bring honour to his name. Lord, even when your path takes me through the valley of deepest darkness, fear will never conquer me, for you already have. You remain close to me and lead me through it all the way. Your authority is my strength and my peace. The comfort of your love takes away my fear. I'll never be lonely, for you are near. You become my delicious feast even when my enemies dare to fight. You anoint me with the fragrance of your Holy Spirit, you give me all I can drink of you until my heart overflows. So why would I fear the future? For your goodness and love pursue me all the days of my life. Then afterward, when my life is through, I'll return to your glorious presence to be forever with you!'

Note also that the devil has a plan which is to steal, kill and destroy (John 10:10a). He works by deceiving, manipulating and controlling.

The only way to overcome the devil is to know The One who is The Truth, The Way, and The Life; Jesus Christ and His Words and align your life with him.

In John 14:6, Jesus said, 'I am the way, the truth, and the life. No one come to the Father except through me'

Jesus Christ of Nazareth is the only way to the true and living God!

Chapter 2

Teenage Years and Early Adulthood

God cares

Although my father and mother have forsaken me, yet the Lord will take me up (adopt me as His own child). (Psalm 27:10. Amplified Bible)

Teach me your ways, O Lord, that I may live according to your truth!

Grant me purity of heart so that I may honour you (Psalms 86: 11. NLT)

Reflecting on this stage in Lily's life (12 to 23), it is amazing how she survived it. It was the most unstable, inconsistent and frustrating season of her life. God must have been keeping and watching over her. That is why the above scripture is very applicable to her experience and she found much comfort in it later in life when she got to know God more.

To begin with, her new father and daddy, David, decided to improve his own life with further study in a University after Lily lived with him for one year. He obtained a scholarship from the government because he was a very brilliant guy. And he had to move into a University campus that was about 649.9 km away from their State. That meant Lily could no longer live with him. He made the arrangement for Lily to live with her older sister, Prosper, and her family. Proper's husband had been transferred from the Northern part of the country to their town just then. David still undertook the responsibility of paying Lily's School fees even though he was a student. He lived a very frugal life so he could save some of his pocket money just to take care of Lily. Prosper and her husband had to provide for Lily with lodging, daily care and other basic needs. Great arrangement! Lily owed them a lot of gratitude.

Lily lived with Prosper and her family in her sixth year in Primary School. Prosper and her husband had two small girls; two years old and under 1 year old then. Lily, always very good with children got attached to the baby so much that she would run after her when she was leaving for School. Sometimes, Lily had to play a hide and seek with her before she could leave for school. Now, Lily looks back to these times with a smile on her face. The children were fun to live with. Prosper later gave birth to their first baby boy while Lily was still living with them. A year after she moved in with them, they were transferred further away. Unfortunately, Lily could not go with them.

Lily moved to live with another relative of her step-sister's husband and family. Here she continued to take care of her step-sister's children. Their mother (Lily's step-sister) was not capable of caring for them anymore due to her mental illness. Their father placed them under the custody of his relatives as he was still being moved around in the army.

He wanted a stable home for his children and needed Lily's help to care for them. He still appreciated how Lily loved and cared for them earlier. Lily had completed her Primary School education by then but had to wait a year before she could start Secondary School. David did not like the Secondary School chosen for Lily by the state, so he advised her to reapply and wait. He had the best in mind for her anyway. He wanted her to attend a grammar school but the state allocated her to a comprehensive school. Though Lily did not really know the difference, she respected his opinion and waited a year out of school.

You may wonder why Lily did not go back to live with her mother. Well, a lot had happened within this period. As mentioned in the previous chapter, her mother did come back to her father's compound about a year after his death. But she was not in a good condition, she had become mentally ill. She was the third person to suffer from mental illness in the family. Being in that condition meant she could not care for her younger children anymore. Her sister adopted her baby, Grace. Elijah was adopted and cared for by some Seminarians in the local Seminary.

At some point while waiting to start Secondary school education, Lily had to go back home to live with her mother. That was when she started to fend for herself. From the pocket money David gave her, she had this idea of trading with it. Talk about learning from her mother even when she was no longer actively teaching her, this was her case. Her goods were peanuts. She bought the raw ones, roasted and took them to the local market. God gave her so much favour; her peanuts sold like hot cake. She would finish her sale before others with the same product in the market. Some customers would even regret they did not come early enough before it finished. From the sales she used to make enough income to buy their food and to re-invest into more raw peanuts. She was now the one caring for her mother. Another job Lily did in this season of her life was working at a petrol (gas) station. She cannot even remember how she got that job. The probability is that she just walked up to that station, it was near to her home and asked the owner for the job. She did not lack even in this very challenging season in her life. She had enough food always, one or two cloths to wear and a pair of slippers. Actually, she had just one dress to go out in, at some point. She would wear it all day and wash and hang it out at night. The hot tropical weather dried it overnight for her to use again the next day. Somehow, she was happy and contented. Her life continued at this pace till she started Secondary School at the age of 14 years.

Eventually, she was admitted into a Grammar School of David's choice. He allowed her to go and made arrangement for her to be in the dormitory as a boarding student. The school was partly a boarding

School, it also had day students. On the first day, Lily went with one of her cousins who was a day student. Lily witnessed how stern the older students were, and how they mal-treated the younger ones when they come late to School. Lily's cousin was made to walk on her knees for about a quarter of a mile because they were late. They were lenient to Lily as a new student. Lily decided never to be late to School again and chose not to go into the boarding house because those older stern students were boarders. She was scared of such treatment. So Lily being always clever, decided to hook up with another cousin who lived close by the School and became a day student. David was not very happy when he found out. But he could not force Lily into the boarding house either, because she had spent some of the money already. Actually, David found out being 'a day student' was cheaper than being a boarder and that Lily was happy. So he let her be. Lily remained in that status till her final year when she decided to go into the boarding house as a senior student to enjoy the privileges.

Lily found out how much the teachers loved and favoured her as soon as she moved into the boarding house. The Girls Senior Prefect elected the previous term was demoted for a very minor incident and Lily was unanimously elected in her place. Being a Senior Prefect was not what Lily really wanted but she could not wiggle out of it. She just had to accept the responsibilities and also the privileges. Up till then, she did not know the tremendous influence she had on both the teachers and students. She was just her quiet studious self, and on top of the class at every years examination result. She was just in her element and happy; love being in School and loved to study. She devoured most books in the library. She was in the Literacy and Debating Club because she loved constructive arguments, and in the Dramatic Club as well. She enjoyed the favour of all her teachers. She never lacked friends but chose her close friends carefully. She was friendly with everybody but had only two close friends. The highlight of her life then was this School period. She loved every bit of being in Secondary School.

However, the challenges were during the holidays. Her daddy, David usually arrange with different family members to pick her up to stay with them during the holidays because he was still in the University. Some kept their promises to him but other would not. Once David came home to find her at home with mother, he was very disappointed with the family member who promised to take her on during that holiday but didn't. For Lily, it was no big deal. She had come to accept life just as it was and learned to thrive no matter her situation. There was a family who lived opposite their compound that she used to go and spent the days with. They had younger children that she used to play with and helped take care of. The couple accepted her and were nice to her. Her daily meals were provided by them. Inevitably, Lily made them her family when she was on holidays.

Life continued at this pace and under this condition until her daddy completed his studies and secured a permanent employment in another town close to their home town. Now, Lily had a home to go to during the holidays until her Secondary school days were over. Once Lily completed her Secondary Education, she wanted to be an independent woman. She was an adult now; 19 years old. Daddy wanted her to live with him until she started University a year after. Their opinions clashed constantly. Lily tricked him by lying to him one day when he was at work. She sent a message to him that she heard their mother was very ill, and she needed to go and see her. Lily locked the house and sent the keys to David by a porter. She got into a public transport and came back to the family home. In order to stop David from taking her away with him when he came home, Lily got herself a job as a sales girl in a Cream Factory. It worked; David came home eventually and could not take Lily away with him. He realised Lily's need for independence as well and left her alone. Lily was happy with herself and the work. Again, Lily had such favour that every time they were taken to the local markets to sell the Creams, she always met her target. Within a few weeks, she was promoted and paid more than the rest of her colleagues. She actually impressed David when next he came home by buying him a nice bottle of wine.

This chapter of Lily's life changed once her GCE result was released, about nine months after the exams. Lily was disappointed with her result; it was six Credits and two Passes. The most unfortunate thing was that the Passes were in English Language and Mathematics, the only subjects mandatory for her admission into a University. Lily's Biology Teacher called her into his office as she was in tears at her result. He expressed his disappointment as well but then tried to encourage her not to be hopeless. He suggested she enroll in Nursing because that result would be accepted there. Lily never wanted to be a nurse. She had two friends who used to wish they could have enough GCE qualifications to enroll in Nursing, but she used to try to discourage them. Lily's desired career was Pharmacy. She told her Biology Teacher this. His response help Lily to change her mind. He said to her, 'My junior sister was taking the same exams as you. If she was qualified, I would have immediately enrolled her into Nursing. You know why? It is free training; you will even be given a bursary while in training to sustain your daily needs. While on this training, you can register for another GCE exams and you can change your mind to pursue your desired career if the result is better. You really have nothing to lose. If you stay at home you will feel bored'. He was a real encourager. Lily went home thinking about his advice and the next day decided to go for it.

'You can make many plans, but the Lord's purpose will prevail' (Proverbs 19:21 NLT)

It was later, when Lily got to know the Lord that she realized the above scripture applied to her situation. Nursing was God's planned career for her and God was ordering her steps into it. At this stage in her life, she did belief there is a God but never thought he was interested in her daily life or future. As it turned out, Lily got to love Nursing, and never got out of it.

So, in response to her Biology Teacher's advice, the next day Lily went to find out about Nursing Registration. To her disappointment, she found out this has already closed. She was referred to a Midwifery School as the registration was currently going on there. The School of Midwifery was about six miles from her home. When she got there, she learnt the registration was closing within the week, and her documents for registration were not complete. She needed what was called 'Age Declaration'. Being born before the war, the birth certificates were destroyed. The only way to confirm her age was by a court declaration. Lily needed someone to do this for her. It so happened that one of her older step-brothers was at home. She went to him for help. He congratulated her on her result, was surprised she wanted to do Nursing, but also very happy to help. The next day, he took her to his barrister friend who drafted it all out, got the necessary signatures and handed Lily her copies. The same day, her step-brother took Lily back to the School of Midwifery for registration. Registration was closed for the day by the time they got there, it was a Friday. Lily was disappointed because the dateline was the next week. And there was an unfriendly cultural event in that part of the community that demanded for all the roads to be blocked. While contemplating on what to do, one of the Tutors came out of the office and Lily recognized her. She was the wife of the medical director of the hospital David worked in. She offered to take Lily's forms and to carry out the registration for her. Was this a coincidence? Lily thought so then but later she did recognize it was God's intervention. This lovely lady completed Lily's registration and she only had to pick up the confirmation at a convenience time.

David got to know all this later when he visited home. He was not happy with Lily's result and with her decision to go into nursing. He had such high expectations for Lily and felt disappointed. However, he could not stop the course of the events unfolding concerning her life and future, so he just let go. Lily had no problem with the entrance exam and interview, they were too simple for her. However, when the list of names of those admitted was published, she was not aware of it. David came home suddenly one weekend and told her. Apparently, he was advised and directed by the husband of the lovely lady Tutor who did Lily's registration to go and meet one of the top personnel handling the admission to see to it that Lily's name was included, as she did not see her name in the admission list. This was Lily's first awareness that corruption does exist, but it did not apply to her case anyway. David said after reporting to these personnel and waiting for action, he decided to look at the admission list and found lily's name right there in the same School that she was registered in. So, he came home straight to tell her, and at the same time resumed his supporting role to Lily. The reasons why this lady did not see Lily's name was because her official name then was different from the one everyone knew her as. You will get to know more about these different names later.

Lily started School of Midwifery in September 1986 It was another exciting time for Lily as she always loved to study. In the class, she was like a sponge, absorbing every theory and devouring the text books in the library. After six months came the first placement in the hospital wards. She was in the male medical ward, and went there with same excitement until on one night duty. The nurse in charge of the shift gave Lily the responsibility to monitor the vital signs of a very ill patient. Lily gave her full attention and care to this patient reporting to the nurse every hour the vital signs. It got to the point she could not detect the patient's radial pulse. When she reported this to the charge nurse, she simply gave Lily the patient's folder and sent her to get the doctor on call. In those days, there were neither bleeps, pager nor phones in the wards to use for the doctor's call. Lily had to walk to the doctors' quarters, knock on the doctor's door and gave him the patient's folder. The doctor came down to the ward immediately and certified the patient dead. It then dawn on Lily, she was handling a death body all this while. She broke out in cold sweat and shivered. She was traumatised. The nurse in charge took no notice of what was going on with this first year, first placement student. Lily's next duty was to go and call the porters to come for the body. She reported to the porters but could not go back to the ward. She went straight to another ward, waited and watched until the corpse was removed from the ward before she went back.

To Lily's surprise, the nurse in charge just said, 'I knew what you did. You should have at least stayed with me and watch how to do the last offices. Next time, you will do it all by yourself'. Lily was horrified to know this is a usual occurrence in the hospital. She felt like quitting but thankfully, this did not happen again during that placement. She actually prayed it would not happen again when she was on duty. It seemed God heard and answered her prayers. In subsequent placements, Lily was in the maternity section. Although she was frightened at the first time she witnessed a delivery, she soon took to midwifery as a duck to water. The birth experiences were awesome, absolute miracles. The joyful expressions of the new parents were infectious. Subsequently, the staff were rewarded with many presents. Lily really got to love the happy environment about it all.

Fast track into Lily's final year in midwifery, a problem developed that opened her understanding to another realm of this life. This will continue in the next chapter....

Chapter 3

Awareness of True and False Spirituality

God is Supernatural

Do you know the devil is also supernatural?

You worship what you do not know; we know what we worship, for salvation is of the Jews (John 4:22 MEV)

Jesus said this to the Samaritan woman He met at the well in a hot Mediterranean afternoon. There is a large statistic of people who worship what they do not know and are very devoted in their worship. Lily's father was certainly one, and he led his whole family into believing a lie, brutal bondage and suffering. And he was very devoted to it even though he did not know what he worshipped and dedicated his life and family to. The question to every reader here is, 'Do you know what you worship?' Do not worry if you are not sure. Keep reading because this book will help you clarify, understand, chose the right God and worship him alone and be blessed.

Here is how the story unfolded; In Midwifery then, students have two exams in the final year. The first was called House Exams, kind of like mock exams because it was marked internally, that is, locally by the School. However, if a student failed these exams, she could not take the final exams which came after six months, but would have to repeat the whole year. It was not a situation any student wanted to be in. Two weeks to this House Exams, the Pastor of the local Apostolic Church (a branch of the church that Lily's mother brought her children up in), Lily and some of the students used to go there, sent to the students to come for prayers. Lily did not go to church that particular Sunday but one of her friends, relayed the message to her. Lily just laughed over it and was not interested. To her, Church then was just like going to a social club. She had no clue of the Spiritual side of it. However, on the day this prayer was scheduled, Lily waved bye to her friends when they left for the prayers, while she collected her books and went to the class to revise. She found myself unable to study. This was very unusual for her. A voice was going on in her mind constantly saying, 'What are you doing here? Do you think you are more intelligent than others who have gone for the prayers?' After some struggle, Lily gave in. Packed her books back to the hostel, got a taxi and went for the prayers. It never occurred to her that God was talking to her. This was Lily's first Spiritual encounter with the supernatural. She arrived just before the prayers started, her friends were surprised to see her but she said nothing to them.

They were about half a dozen students. They were surrounded by members of the church prayer group and they began to pray and prophecy over the students. One of the prophetic words was,

'Oh you from a strong family! Two outcomes awaits you; it is either you fail the exams and live, or pass and die! Oh! The stomach ache that you will have during the exams will cause you to be carried out of the exams hall. However, if you draw close to me, I will deliver you'

At that time, Lily had no idea what these words meant. The pastor at the end of the prayers counselled them to dedicate their lives to the Lord by abstaining from sinful habits and activities (stay away from your boyfriends was one), and to fast and pray. This happened on a Sunday evening, three days before the exams start. The following day, a Monday, Lily just felt like acting on the pastor's advice. So she decided to fast and pray. Her roommate had interestingly decided to prepare a very enticing breakfast that same morning. She was surprised when Lily said 'no' but Lily chose to resist the temptation. She took her books to the class, study till 12 noon, and just prayed a simple prayer of committing her life and the exams to God. She did the same the next day being a Tuesday and the next, Wednesday, which was the exams day.

She then went into the exams hall with a fast.

As soon as Lily finished answering all her exams questions, she began to experience a kind of dull stomach ache. She thought might be she was hungry at first. She went to the hostel and had some food, but the ache did not stop. The practical part of the exams was starting the next day, a Thursday. Lily decided to go to town to get her hair done so she will appear smart for the practical exams. The town was about six miles away. Lily went by taxi. After having her hair done, she became thirsty before she left the salon and asked the hair dresser for a drink. The hair dresser happily brought her a glass of water which she drank. As soon as she finished this drink, a terrible pain rose from her stomach and exploded in her chest. Lily fell down unconscious and was in that position for about four hours. By the time she resumed consciousness, her hair dresser was alone watching over her, frightened and lost. Her only hope was that Lily was breathing normally. She was greatly relieved when Lily resumed consciousness. In this part of the world, there was no ambulance to call. It was around midnight when Lily came back to herself. She was determined to go back to School because of her impending practical exams the next day. The hair dresser called a taxi for her. The driver started to play up with Lily after she got into the taxi. He asked Lily to come and spend the night with him, promising to drop her off in the morning. Lily got mad with him and commanded him to drop her by the main road that was on her way. He obliged, and Lily waited there flagging down any car that came. God had mercy on Lily; the first car that stopped was a Seminarian, who was my Elijah's friend.

He was surprised to see Lily at that time of the night there and also very happy to take her back to the hostel.

The stomach ache continued as a dull ache till in the morning. Lily could not have a proper sleep. Guest what? She was the first to be call in for the practical exams that Thursday morning. She did not expect to be the first as the candidates surnames were sorted alphabetically and her surname began with U. So, she was trying to rest a bit more in the morning and was not ready. The Vice Principal went to the hostel, found her in pains and ordered her mates to take her to the hospital ward for admission. She then encouraged Lily to be ready to take her practical the next day being a Friday because there was no resist in these exams and being one of the bright students, she did not want Lily to miss this opportunity. Lily spent the night in the hospital ward. All investigations results were negative. She was kept on Buscopan (analgesia) and Valium (Diazepam) injections to control the pain. Finally, Lily slept and had a good night. The next morning, Friday, she asked the nurse to give her only Buscopan injection so she could stay alert. She went to the hostel, got herself ready and went and did the practical exams. Lily was successful. Guess what? The pain never came back throughout the day. In the evening, she was discharged from the ward. That was when she realised the prophecy in the Church Prayer meeting was for me.

This event opened Lily's awareness in the following ways:

- She began to wonder what made her family 'a strong' one.

- Somehow, she sensed it had to do with her father's church but had no clarity at this stage.

- She realized life is not all about what we see; there is another realm that we do not see. And what goes on there definitely manifest in the natural. This is the Spiritual realm, it is supernatural.

- Her perspective of The Apostolic Church changed; The God worshiped here is real and good. He even spoke to her and answered her simple prayers.

- She became thankful to this good God that helped her pass the exams and live. Going to church was no more like going to a social club. Lily became aware of God's presence in the gatherings of His people. The singings and prayers began to convey deeper meanings than they did previously.

A month after this, another event occurred in Lily's life. She began to experience a kind of headache; it started as a migraine and gradually increased to the level she needed hospital admission because it was not relieved by common analgesia. For two weeks in the hospital, Lily underwent various investigations, blood tests and even lumbar puncture. All results were negative. The doctors did not know what to do with her case. At this stage, Lily was unable to eat, sleep or take care of herself.

She was totally dependent on the care of nursing staff.

Lily's friend went to the same Apostolic Church who prayed for them last time to ask for prayers for Lily. Again, the prayer group fixed a date and time and her friend helped her to get there. Thank God for good friends. They are indispensable. The encouragement to the reader now is to stop and ask God for good friends if you do not have any. Also to try to be a good friend to someone. A lonely life is the most miserable and dangerous life for anyone to live. We need each other.

In the Church, the prayer group members stood in a circle around Lily and prayed. Another prophetic word came:

'My child, your problem is not a hospital one. The strong man has bound you and is hitting your head hard. His aim is to kill you or to make you mental. But I will deliver you if you draw close to me'

This time around, Lily believed the word and took it seriously. When she got back to the hospital ward, she asked to be discharge against medical advice. The medical personnel did not want to discharge her because she was still very ill. Lily had to send for her older step-brother who was available. He came and signed the necessary papers and took her to his pastor's home. This step-brother was a Born-Again believer, so he understood Spiritual things. David, her daddy did not believe and thought her case outside the hospital was hopeless. Lily later understood this step-brother had similar experiences that he overcame through prayers. His pastor and wife were happy to have Lily in their home. As soon as this pastor prayed for Lily, the headache lifted off. Lily felt well, sat up and was hungry. She requested for food and they gave her something to eat. She ate for the first time in two weeks. In the hospital, she was kept alive on Intravenous infusions and morphine. She was too drowsy to eat. Here she felt better and slept better that night. The next morning, the pastor said to Lily,

'I had thought it was an ordinary headache when I prayed for you. I realised it was not because the enemy attacked me in the night. But you don't have to worry, Jesus is stronger than the devil, and you are safe'

Indeed, Lily felt well and safe for a couple of days that the pastor was at home. The following week the pastor went on a ministry trip that took him away from home. From the time the pastor left in the morning, Lily was tormented with the headache again. By the evening of that same day, she was very afraid. The pastor's wife was at home. She prayed for Lily but she was not as spiritually aware or strong like her husband. Her prayers were not so effective. Lily realised there are some believers presence that the devil will not mess up with, and there are those he can play games with. So she decided to take herself out of that house, got a taxi and went to the local branch of The Apostolic Church that she knew. She believed God was planning this for her because there was a prayer meeting in full session as she stepped into the church, and immediately, the headache vanished. Lily was not even prayed for then. At the end of the prayer meeting, Lily shared her problem with the leading elder of the church. He encouraged her to stay in the church with daily fasting till 12 midday. Lily complied. Every day, and at noon, the elder prayed for Lily. She began to have a funny sensation in her body; the pain moved around from her head to her neck, then to her shoulder, back, waist and down to her feet. Lily kept reporting these sensations to the elder. He just reassured her every time that the pain is on its way out. And he was right. After about one month, Lily was pain free.

Wow! Lily was so thankful to God. To show this thankfulness, she decided to share testimony on the Sunday evening gathering of the week that she began to feel well. Her intention was to return to School on the

Monday following to resume her studies and prepare for the final exams.

After giving this testimony, another prophecy came from the elder's wife; 'My child, do not be careless. What is in front of you is worse than what you have gone through. Stay close to me so I can give you continuous victory'

Lily was devastated on hearing these prophetic words. Her cousin who was taking care of her at this time, because she was in the church, said to Lily, 'Do not bother about that prophecy. This elder's wife talks too much so her prophetic word cannot be trusted'. However, Lily knew the word was true because even though she felt better, she struggled with her studies. Her friends have been visiting her in the church and brought some of her text books to encourage her to study as their final exams was fast approaching; just a few months away. But every time she attempted to read, her head felt so heavy, she just had to put the book down. This experience made her believed the prophetic word though she did not fully understand it. She thought 'stay close to me' meant stay in the church. At the end of the meeting, she went to the elder and told him she could not go back to School as she had no hope of being able to study. She decided she would just stay in the church if that was how her life would be spared. Thank God this man of God had a great spiritual awareness and understanding. He looked at Lily and said,

'Don't worry. All you need to do is fast for three days from food and water. I will pray for you at the end of the fast and you will have your total deliverance and will be able to go back to your study'.

Lily wondered whether she would survive another fasting season, and voiced it out. Already, she looked like just skin and bones from all the fast. His response was, 'A big roast needs a huge fire'.

Lily felt encouraged and commenced the fast the next day. Her cousin prepared her with fresh coconut drinks. At midday on the third day, this elder placed his hands on Lily's head and declared,

'In the Name of Jesus, I remove the family burden put on you and shatter it now'.

Lily felt a heavy weight lifted off her head and she was free! Hallelujah!!! She went back to School the next day, enjoyed her revisions and passed the final exams with good grade in just a month.

Lily's awareness in this season:

- Jesus is not just in history. He is alive and well and His name is powerful. He is able to deliver from the devil's bondage.

- God intervenes in our lives for good even when we do not know Him.

- God can speak to you through unusual people and circumstances, but you will be able to confirm in your spirit the authenticity of the prophetic words.

- Lily now had definite conviction her father was worshipping the devil in the name of a church. By now he has been dead for over 16 years, his church was no longer in operation in the family. Lily wondered how it still had such influence.

- Things began to fit like a jigsaw puzzle to Lily: her older step-sister's mental illness, her mother's mental illness, and Noah's dysfunctional life. There was another younger step-sister with mental illness as well whose mother, her father's first wife, was like a deaconess and still lived in the headquarters of her father's church. It was quite a complicated puzzle but Lily sensed all these problems in her family had a linked to their father's church.

- Lily embarked on a quest to understand this mystery and to fight for her mother's deliverance. She desperately wanted her mother back. She believed the God that delivered her could deliver her mother as well.

As soon as Lily was financially established, she took her mother out of the family house to a branch of The Apostolic Church that held a healing home for people, left her there and supported her for months. Sad to say her deliverance did not happen as Lily expected. However, she persevered.

Chapter 4

The Born-Again Experience and Life

Jesus replied, 'I tell you the truth, unless you are born again, you cannot see the Kingdom of God' (John 3:3 NLT)

At this stage in Lily's life, she had tasted the goodness of God. She believed in Him, but did not understand the scriptures. The above scripture made no meaning to her then. She knew some people who claimed to be born again, even one of her step-sisters and a step-brother were among this group. However, Lily did not see any difference between their lives and others' except that they went to a different church they used to jokingly in the family called The Born-Again Church.

Lily loved God though, because she had experienced his goodness. She expressed this love by going more to The Apostolic Church and taking part in as many activities as she possibly could. She learned to trust this God with her life and future. When she had the opportunity, as some of her colleagues, to choose where she wanted to work after her qualification as a Midwife, she decided to leave the decision in God's hands by praying about it. She believed God was able to take care of her. When the posting list was released, only Lily and another one of her colleagues were sent to this unusual Health Centre that none of them has ever heard of. At first they thought it was a mistake because they did not know where it was or how to get there. The rest of their colleagues felt the same except one. This colleague came around and declared she and her husband passed by the Health Centre one day on their way to somewhere. She told them it was a new Health Centre in a particular local government area about 20 miles from their School.

Finally, they knew the location. This colleague also proceeded to give them the direction. This was a wonderful relief to Lily and her colleague.

Armed with this information, they made their way down to this Health Centre and commenced their first time employment as midwives. The transition from student to a qualified midwife was exciting. This first posting turned out to be very good as well. They had a modern two bedroom bungalow to share and a plot of land to cultivate, all free. Attending to the local women was a pleasure. However, they worked around the clock as they were resident midwives. There was a matron who also had a bungalow in the centre but she was not residing there much. These young midwives developed fast and became very independent and competent in managing the local women from prenatal to delivery and puerperium, and even home visits and immunizations. They were loved by the locals also; being the first midwives they ever had. Treating their minor injuries and ailments was also part of the midwives' role. Life felt good and stress free to these young midwives. They were able to screen cases properly in early pregnancy, managed those they were competent with and refer the complex cases to the nearest hospital.

The following year, two more staff were sent to the centre; a new midwife and a double qualified staff (double qualified meant she was qualified both as a General Nurse and a Midwife). The double qualified was immediately recognized as the assistant manager of the Centre, and she was resident as well.

Something interesting happened; she became friendly with Lily. She used to go over to her bungalow. They cooked, ate and played games together whenever they were not at work. Her name was Lovett. Lovett was married and also claimed to be a born-again believer. Lily's first impression of her was that she was very friendly, unlike other born-again believers that she knew. Lovett never tried preaching to Lily, occasionally, she would mention being 'born again', and Lily would say to her, 'I will think about it after enjoying my life'. She just smiled and changed the subject. They just remained very good friends with each other.

Life continued in this pace until somehow, the local council decided to charge them for the accommodation, and they made the charges very expensive. The staff decided to vacate the accommodation. Lovett was from that locality, and had a friend who lived about two miles away. She reasoned with Lily; they could get a cheaper accommodation in the town, and ride to work on local public transport. The Health Centre was just on the main road, very easy to access. This would save them a lot of money. There were other problems at the centre also between management and staff, so relocation was just inevitable. It was like a storm in their nest, and they had to flee to safety.

They all went in different directions. Lovett and Lily shared an apartment initially in the town with Lovett's friend, who was also a born again young man and they were in the same born again Church. One evening, their Pastor visited. After the usual introduction, pleasantry and chatting, he looked Lily in the eye and asked,

'Are you a child of God?'

Lily responded, 'Yes, of course'.

He chatted about other things and then came back to Lily and asked,

'Are you free from sin?'

Lily laughed at him and said, 'Is there anybody who is free from sin? Are we not all sinners saved by God's grace?'

See, Lily did know that scripture; that was the one preach most in her Church, The Apostolic Church. It is sad to say though, that despite the great demonstration of the power and the grace of God in this Church, the leaders did not preach the total truth and did not encourage the members to live free from sin. One of the prevalent sin was sexual sin, most leaders practice adultery and to the young people having your boyfriend or girlfriend and indulging in sex before marriage was okay. And Lily was the same. However, this pastor's next question shook Lily to the core; he said,

'Do you believe the Bible?'

Lily responded, 'Yes'.

He said, 'If I show you from the Bible that you can be free from sin, would you believe?'

Lily said, 'Yea, go on'. And handed him her Bible. He opened and then read;

'Little children, let no one deceive you. The one who does righteousness is righteous, just as Christ is righteous. Whoever practices sin is of the devil, for the devil has been sinning from the beginning. For this purpose, the Son of God was revealed, that He might destroy the works of the devil. Whoever has been born of God does not practice sin, for His seed remains in him. And he cannot keep on sinning, because he has been born of God. In this the children of God and the children of the devil are revealed: Whoever does not live in righteousness is not of God, nor is the one who does not love his brother'. (1 John 3:7-10)

Lily could not believe what she heard when he finished the reading. 'Is that in my Bible?' she asked. He responded with a definite 'Yes' and handed the Bible to her to read for herself. Lily was heavily convicted when she read these words. She remembered the goodness of God when he healed and freed her from the wickedness of the devil who wanted to kill her. Felt the shame and guilt of living like the devil's child.

With tears streaming down her face, she said, 'My sins are too much,

God will not forgive me'.

This sensitive and compassionate man of God responded, 'Let me tell you a story; Suppose you have a child who is very rebellious, left home without your permission and doesn't even care about what you say or think. Then one day this child comes back and is deeply sorry for his behaviour and wants to come back home, won't you forgive and accept him back?' Lily responded, 'Of course, I would, and that's my child'. The man of God responded, 'Well you are God's child, that's how He sees you. Do you want to come home now?' Lily responded, 'How?' He proceeded to lead Lily in a prayer of repentance and Lily surrendered her life to God by inviting Jesus into her heart. The impact was awesome, Lily felt a heavy weight lifted off her shoulders as she prayed. At the end, she felt such an incredible peace and joy.

The man of God concluded with these words, 'Welcome home! You are now a Born-Again believer'. Lily was like, Wow! She never thought this was real. Experiencing this was so surreal to her. She felt like walking on the cloud. She literally experienced the joy of heaven as recorded in this scripture:

'In the same way, there is more joy in heaven over one lost sinner who repents and returns to God…..'(Luke 17:7 NLT).

Lily's life was transformed. This pastor became her Spiritual Father. He adopted Lily into his family as his oldest daughter. His wife and children loved and accepted Lily also as part of the family. Together with Lovett and her friend, they continued with the work of nurturing, teaching and feeding Lily with The Word of God, and meeting her practical needs as they were able. Lily grew speedily as well in her ability to study and understand The Word and in devouring other Christian literatures. Lily had so much hunger for The Word and found reading the Bible in the morning and at bedtime very fulfilling.

Another person who helped Lily in her spiritual journey was Lovett friend's brother. He was a Pastor too. He lived a distance away and used to visit them. He was a very good counsellor, had an in-depth attitude to listen, understand and helped Lily in making difficult decisions. One of these decisions was breaking off from the relationship that she had been in for over two years. Just before this born again experience, her fiancé had proposed marriage and she had accepted. The next plan was for Lily to introduce him to her family for the necessary marriage traditional rites and ceremony. They had in mind to do that in December, but and Lily became born again in October of the same year. Part of Lily felt it was a narrow escape from a possible miserable future (marriage was a very scary venture to Lily anyway because of all the unhappy and miserable marriages she had witness in her younger life especially her mother's and Prosper's marriages. However, Lily was very indebted to her fiancé and felt guilty breaking up the relationship. He had cared for her while in the School of Midwifery and through her most difficult times.

He also helped her to become established and settled in her first posting. Part of Lily thought he really loved her but the other part of her was very confused.

This Pastor happened to visit Lily on one of her confused days. By this time Lily had secured her own apartment and moved into it. The Pastor listened attentively to Lily without interruption and at the end just said, 'I cannot tell you not to marry or marry him. What I can tell you is that you are at a higher spiritual level now than him. In marriage, the man is your leader. It will be easier for him to pull you down to his level than for you to pull him up to yours. And that can create a constant conflict in your relationship'. He then prayed with Lily and asked God to help her make the right decision. And God did give Lily the wisdom that helped detangled her from that relationship. She felt like writing to inform her fiancé of her born-again experience and desire not to continue as they were before. To Lily's surprise, her fiancé became very angry after receiving her letter, accused Lily of blackmailing him and demanded she return all his gifts to her. Lily had never seen him angry for the two years they had been in the relationship, his anger was not reasonable either, to her surprise. Lily negotiated with an elder in her Church who was aware of and encouraging the relationship, returned what she could to the fiancé, some in money value. He prayed with them and broke up the engagement. After this, Lily cherished her freedom the more. She chose the love of Jesus and focus on Him alone. Jesus was everything to Lily. Her everyday adventure with Him had been and is always unusual, but Lily loved it all. There is no boring moment with Jesus Christ of Nazareth; the Son of God.

Lily felt led by the Holy Spirit as time went on to Scripture Union where she was trained via interactive Bible study, literatures, and daily Bible study guides, and in fasting and prayers. This ministry used to organize three days fasting and prayer conferences yearly, and other conferences as well. Lily engaged in these activities and found attending these conferences a great time of Spiritual refreshment, growth and aspirations. It was a season of accelerated Spiritual growth for this Baby Christian as she fed on the milk of the Word of God and in fellowship with mature believers.

Lily was surrounded with lovely and sincere believers in this season of her life.

Among them were:

- Lovett, her husband and children.

- Her father in the Lord and his wife, (whom she fondly called Daddy & Mommy), and their family.

- Lovett's friend, a lovely Christian brother. Lily lived with him for a while, about two months, after her initial conversion, and before she moved to her own rented house. Lily got to know that a young man can be truly saved and set free from lust through living with him. He was a true brother in Christ. He taught Lily how to study the Bible daily and pray accordingly. Lily slept in the same bed with him at nights and he never took advantage of her. Lily become convinced the born-again life was possible to both genders through her relationship with this wonderful brother. He now has is family.

- They all remain close to Lily's heart.

- Two lovely sisters were Lily's closest prayer partners and confidants; Gift and Flo.

The love and care from these people gave Lily the blissful experience of belonging to God's family on earth. She became closer and more open to these members of the Body of Christ than she was to her biological family. Indeed, the ties that bound her to this family of God was stronger than the biological. God's love flowing through humans is the best kind of love.

Lily's awareness in this season:

- As humans, we were made for relationship. In the natural, we relate with one another as families or friends. We cannot grow and thrive without these relationships.

- As humans, we are not just the physical that we can see, we are spiritual beings; the part of us that we cannot see.

- As spiritual beings, we yearn for spiritual relationship so we can grow and thrive. That's why we worship. That is what religion is all about; humans seeking to relate spiritually.

- Unfortunately, some in their search ended up in relating to the wrong spirituality which is the devil and his demons. Lily's father was in this category, and this relationship brought much distress into his life and family because all the devil comes to do is steal, kill and destroy humans and the purposes of God in them.

- 'The thief's purpose is to steal and kill and destroy' (John 10:10a. NLT).

- The devils strategy is deception, manipulation, control and destruction of the human race because he hates us. You may ask, 'What about the atheist?' I believe they worship somehow, it may be things or themselves, this is still wrong relationship / worship. The worst tragedy in life is for anyone to live and die in deception.

- The right spiritual relationship is in getting to know Jesus in a personal way by surrendering one's life to Him. When we open our lives to Him, He comes in to give us life in abundance;

Jesus says:

> *'My purpose is to give them a rich and satisfying life' (John 10:10b. NLT).*

- This life flows from our spirits as we connect with Him and influences our emotional, mental, physical life and relationships.

- Unfortunately, some people can be in the church and just remain religious; not having the spiritual relationship with God through

- Jesus. That's where Lily was before. Jesus did not die for us to just be religious. He died so we can enter into a relationship with God, and live out of our true spiritual nature.

- When we are just religious, we are unstable spiritually and lack spiritual understanding. We are easily influenced by other people's opinions and live from the outside in, depending on people's approval. This is not the abundant life Jesus came to give us.

- In relationship with Jesus, we get to know our true identity. This is very crucial in living life with purpose and meaning and in finding fulfilment in what we do because we live from the inside out, from the place of inspiration. Life becomes a daily adventure. There is no place for boredom here.

Lily's quest for her mother's freedom

Lily in this season was desperate for her mother to be delivered. As soon as she settled down at her place of work and before her born-again experience, she got her mother out of the family home to another branch of The Apostolic Church that had a home for people with different kind of illnesses. The people were housed there while being ministered to with prayers and at times with fasting until they were healed. Lily cannot remember how long her mother stayed there. All she can remember is that a few months after her born-again experience, she decided her mother needed this experience as well.. It would certainly be better for her than just being religious which was what she has been all of her life, Lily thought. So she took the next step of getting her out of this healing home and brought mother to live with her. Lily wanted her mother exposed to this atmosphere of born-again believers, prayer and Bible study style of living. Mother obliged to all of these. Lily's friends were very nice, compassionate and helpful in praying for and helping Lily take care of her. Mother gradually got better physically with good nutrition and became more self-aware mentally. With the self-awareness came the desire to do something, to be active, because she was bored. Someone advised Lily to buy her some melon seed to peel. She was quite happy peeling these melon seeds. A neighbour who ran a restaurant saw her peeling these seeds and offered to buy them. With the sale, they made an interest of 90%. A mini business commenced and they had more than enough finances and were living comfortably.

Prior to the above financial breakthrough, Lily had some financial difficulties. Her monthly salary was not enough to sustain her mother's care as well as her little sister - Grace's Secondary School fees. By this time, she was led by the Holy Spirit to move to a Church that prioritized teaching of the Word of God, The Assemblies of God Church. The pastor taught one Sunday on tithing in a way that Lily was convicted. Lily went back home and read the scripture again:

'Bring all the tithes into the storehouse so there will be enough food in my Temple. If you do, 'says the Lord of Heaven's Armies, 'I will open the window of heaven for you. I will pour out a blessing so great you won't have enough room to take it in! Try it! Put me to the test!

'Your crops will be abundant, for I will guard them from insects and disease. Your grapes will not fall from the vine before they are ripe', says the Lord of Heaven Armies'.

'Then all nations will call you blessed, for your land will be such a delight', says the Lord of Heaven Armies' (Malachi 3: 10 – 12)

At the end of that year, Lily made a resolution to start to pay her tithe in the New Year. When she received her January salary, she first took out the tithe, opened her bible and read the above scripture again and said to the Lord, 'I will trust and try you on this'. She gave the money as offering in Church the following Sunday. By the time she paid her rent and electric bills, and gave Grace her School fees, she had only about 50 dollars left for food and other basic needs for the month. This would have lasted just one week in those days but God did a miracle. An unusual visitor came to her house, saw her mother and before leaving gave her 50 dollars. It was this money that Lily used to buy her mother the melon seeds to peel. After the initial 90% interest, both Lily and her mother recognized the source of this blessing. They gave tithe and offerings from the interest, invest the remaining and the business grew. Lily learnt that God wants to bless us but sometimes can only do it if we chose to believe and obey his word. Lily was two years old as a born-again believer in this season.

About a year later, Lily was transferred to a more remote part of the community where she could not take mother with her. Her beloved brothers and sisters in Christ prayed for the transfer to be cancelled but it was not. Lily was distressed by this transfer especially for her mother as she had no other option but to return her back to the family home. Lily felt her mother was making progress because she was encouraging her. At home, there was no body to do that. David was working from home by then but he was not interested in God at all, and would not encourage her accordingly. However, Lily had no choice but to return her home and she did eventually. Lily's fear was confirmed when she visited home about a month after; her mother had gone down mentally. Lily was in distress and wept for days. However, at some point, she felt comforted by the Holy Spirit.

Lesson Lily learn after this season:

- That was her best effort to make things happened but it was not God's way.

- The right way would have been to seek God first, hear from Him and act accordingly.

- Her mother's problem was more than her limited comprehension. Lily had allowed her desire for mother's healing to become an idol, took her focus away from her relationship with God. God in his mercy has allowed the transfer so as to break Lily off this wrong focus, which could have empowered the devil. Anything that takes first place in our lives, consumes our desire is idolatry.

- Lily became aware her only responsibility was to stay focus on God, and to enjoy His love.

One day as she studied the Bible, these words impacted her;

I am the Lord, the God of all the peoples of the world. Is anything too hard for me? Jeremiah 32:27

As Lily reflected on these words, God assured her. He understood her anguish, has heard her prayers and will answer in His timing and in His own way. All Lily had to do was to trust Him.

Lily was comforted. Rose up from her ashes of disappointment, guilt and condemnation that she had failed God and her mother, and refocused on God's love for her. Her perspective changed; she learned to pray, 'Lord, not my will, but yours be done!'

Lily had peace! And as she kept walking with the Lord, her spiritual understanding began to open to the network of evil in their family.

The first understanding Lily had was that her step-mother, her father's first wife, was still orchestrating the demonic worship and its effects in the family. She was still living at the headquarters as her husband wanted her to do and operating from there. Lily understood she has drawn her mother into it and made her to be operating from the family home. Her mother was made mentally ill because she did not willingly accept to be part of it. She was just being used, a kind of spiritual abuse and a scape goat. Lily shared this revelation with two of her older step-sisters, who were born-again believers long before her. One did not understand it at all but one did and they agreed to pray for God to uproot this headquarters which was the stronghold of the demonic worship. After praying for a while, Lily's step-brother, the only son of this step-mother suddenly visited Lily at her place of work. He also has been a born-again Christian for years. He stayed for a few days with Lily and as they interacted, this conversation came up. The Lord opened his understanding also; his sister was the first to have mental illness in the family. They used to blame the husband for it but one day; the husband told them his father in-law confessed God was punishing his daughter and that he should leave her. The poor man had no choice but to do as the father in-law instructed him: left his wife. So Lily's step-brother recalled this and believed the revelation. He joined in the prayers.

A few months after, God acted; the villagers attacked this demonic community and everyone was running for their lives. Lily's step-sister went to visit the mother just in time, found her hiding in the bush, informed the brother and they went and collected her. This woman used to tell her children she would die in that place but this time around she willingly followed them out of there. God moved in response to their prayers.

However, this was not the end of the story, they all wished it was. More about this later.

The second revelation Lily had was about her name. Remember, she mentioned having two names before; one was used by all the members of the family. This name was Lily. There was controversy on who gave her this name in the family. Lily's understanding was that her grandmother gave her this name but later Prosper said she was the one.

Their grandmother died shortly after Lily's birth. Lily used this name up to Primary 3. When she moved to live with her father from Primary 4, he changed the name officially to the name he gave her. This name was

Message. He used to fondly called God's Message. The Lord revealed to Lily that her father covenanted this name to his god, the devil, and the devil has a legal hold on her because of the name. Lily had to change this name. This was a difficult thing to do because all her certificates carried this name. However, the Lord made a way for her. The following year, Lily had to go back for her further qualification: in General Nursing. She used this opportunity to change the name. Lily had this weird feeling of increased freedom after this name change that was and still is hard to explain. She sailed through her training smoothly and got her qualification without any event a year and half after. The truth was; the devil had no legal hold on her and could not block her anymore. This was an amazing experience to Lily.

It was like what Jesus said in John 14:30

'I don't have much more time to talk to you, because the ruler of this world approaches. He has no power over me' (NLT)

To conclude this chapter, the encouragement to the reader is to focus on Jesus, enjoy His grace and the Father's love. Every other thing in your life will align for your own good. He will show you where they are blockages in your life as a result of past traumas, abuse or unrighteous covenants. Just work with him and the people he brings into your life to help you, he will show you how to remove these blockages so you can have the abundant life He died for you to have. This God is a very good Father who has good plans for His children. Trust him and you will enjoy your adventures with Him!

Chapter 5

Marriage

Marriage was a no go area for Lily before her born-again experience because of all the abuse she saw in the marriages in her family and those around her. In her early adult life, men who had her attention were not just interested in her but able to pursue her relentlessly. She did get to realise this is the nature of all men; they pursue to conquer. Lily had few boyfriends and was okay on a friendly level until they crossed the barrier by venturing to ask her for marriage. As soon as that happened, the door to the relationship just shut. Lily was very good in studying people and expert in spotting all the things that are wrong in their behaviour and attitudes. She was looking for the perfect man. Unfortunately, they do not exist. Interestingly, Lily never thought she was perfect either.

You can recall in the previous chapter, a two-year relationship that Lily had to let go when she became born-again. This was one of those series of men who pursued her till she felt maybe he really loved her and was different, and then gave him a chance. For two years, Lily studied this man but could not crack him open. He was always calm and calculated, never reacted to all her attempts to unruffled him. He was the only one that came close to having her heart but unfortunately, he showed Lily the nasty part of him after the breakup; further confirming her fears. After this, Lily resolved to focus on Jesus' love.

Sadly, even the Christian marriages that Lily came in contact with after her born-again experience did not inspire her either. At a closer level, she could still spot the selfishness in the men. However, she was freer with the Christian men as she saw them as her Spiritual brothers. Sadly, some of the single men misinterpreted her friendliness and ventured to ask her for marriage, and felt rejected when her response was not what they expected. Lily just felt she could not help them and kept moving on with her life.

However, Lily's world was rocked at the age of 27 years. That was when Stanley, the man she eventually married first made his intentions known to her. Prior to this, they were living in the same compound for over three years, worked together at the same place of work for about two years and worshipped together in the same Church for about two years. So they did interact a lot. One of the things Lily particularly liked about Stanley was his faith and the ability to teach The Word of God with clarity.

It happened when the Lord directed Lily to move from The Apostolic Church to Assemblies of God which was Stanley's Church. Of all the Sunday School Teachers in this Church, he was the best. Lily was drawn to the anointing in him because his teachings were clear and applicable in life. She used to upset the single ladies' Teacher whose class she was meant to always attend by switching classes to wherever Stanley taught. The thought of marriage to him never crossed her mind though. As usual, during their interactions outside the Church, she had also become aware of things in him that would potentially make marriage to him a disaster.

One day, they were at work together. Stanley's cousin brought him some beans cakes. He ate it all right in front of Lily without even sharing a piece with her. In that culture, that was a terrible expression of selfishness. But just when he had finished the eating, a question popped into Lily's mind; 'What if this man asked you for marriage?' Lily responded, 'Over my dead body. Who would ever marry someone as selfish as this?' And the next word she heard was, 'You will be dead indeed by then'. Lily had no clue this conversation was with God. She thought this man is trying to play charismatic witchcraft on her. With this thought, she proceeded to tell him a story about charismatic witchcraft in the most recent book that she read just to warn him. She hoped he understood and that ended the case. Later that year, Lily left that place of work for her double qualification training.

One day, Stanley turned up in her School which happened to be his previous School of Nursing to collect some documents. He then told Lily he is moving abroad for work. Lily was happy for him and congratulated him. Suddenly he said her, 'I will come for you when I am settled'. Lily responded, 'I'm not interested in living abroad but in the dollars if you can share some'. Lily thought he was joking and was responding accordingly. By the end of that month, Lily came back to her place of work to collect her salary. The training was in-service with full pay but they had to go to the Local Council where the Hospital was to collect their cheques at the end of the month.

Stanley came to her house when he knew she was around and actually made his intentions clear. Lily was angry with him because he actually used the word, 'God revealed to me that you are my wife'. He did not know Lily had already heard he was going around with his Pastor to different branches of the Church for wife hunting. Lily was also disappointed in him as a spiritual person for being that confused. So she gave him a piece of her mind in a way that was not pleasant. Stanley was speechless and moved broad without any further contact with her. Lily was okay with that.

The next year, Stanley came back and again went wife hunting. Lily heard about it and was not bothered. However, for the sake of old friendship, she decided she would attend his wedding. In this culture, you can just turn up for a wedding party even if you were not invited and no one would stop you. Lily first went to one of her friends who was also Stanley's friend to find out when and where his wedding would be. To her surprise, the friend said he did not succeed in getting the marriage sorted and has gone back abroad. Though this was not a funny story, Lily found herself laughing. Just then, she heard a rebuke on the inside and knew it was the Lord. The Lord said, 'Don't laugh because I am the one blocking his path'. Lily responded, 'But why?' The Lord continued, 'Because you are my will for him'. Lily responded, 'But he does not see it. Besides he does not even love me. Why would you give me to a man like that?' The Lord responded, 'Because there is a blockage that is preventing him. I want you to wait on me'. The conversation stopped there and Lily understood what that 'wait on me' meant. Her friend noticed she was quiet and asked what she was thinking. Lily refused to share these conversations with the Lord with her because she knew her friend will not keep it confidential. So, she distracted her friend with something else and spent the weekend with her as she intended.

When she resumed work after the weekend, Lily went to another friend, her prayer partner whom she could trust with confidentiality and shared her secret. Lily requested for her guest room where she waited on the Lord with fasting and prayer for three days. This prayer partner also prayed with her about the issue. After this, Lily felt the burden to pray lift. She went about her daily activities with a renewed sense of peace, no more plagued with these marriage thoughts.

Lily completed her double qualification training a year after above incidence and returned to full time work in the same place of work and community. During this time, other potential suitors were coming to ask her for marriage. The Assemblies of God Church had a system that prohibits the single men from approaching the ladies directly for marriage. They had to go through the Pastor of the church in which the girl they fancy worshiped. Some Pastors actively campaign for and match-make the singles in their congregations and across congregations. Lily did experience all these. She had one Pastor who was exasperated with her because her responses were always 'No'. He was worried she was becoming an old maid as she was missing her chances. At some point, Lily had to avoid him. When she was returning to work, she made a deal with the Lord to relocate her or the Pastor.

The Lord chose to relocate the Pastor, so Lily returned to the same Church. The new Pastor was a more considerate man. He would tell Lily to go and pray about any man who came to him to ask for her. He wanted Lily to hear from the Lord by herself. Lily loved and respected him greatly for this. Then at some point when Lily's response was always 'No' even to men who felt they had the revelation from the Lord, and his wife had a dream she thought confirmed same, this Pastor called Lily into his home and had an honest discussion with her. It went like this;

Pastor: Sister, what really is the Lord telling you to do? Does he want you to stay single and serve Him?

Lily: Not really. He has shown me His will for me in marriage.

Pastor: Where is he?

Lily: He is abroad.

Pastor: Does he know?

Lily: I don't know.

Pastor: Why don't you tell him?

Lily: Never, the Lord has to do it.

This pastor never bothered Lily again with the issue but would tell any man who came to him thereafter to forget it. His wife was actually different. On one occasion, she told Lily she had a dream about her and a particular man exchanging rings and was convinced he was God's will in marriage for Lily. When Lily responded with the fact that she needs her own personal conviction, the pastor's wife said, 'Sister, what if the

Lord reveals it to every other person?' Lily responded, 'Well, every other person is not me'. The case was then closed.

At the end of that year 1995, Stanley came back home for his mother's burial. He went straight to Lily and re-proposed. By now, Lily was 'dead' indeed and her response was a definite 'Yes'. She realised the phrase, 'Dead to self' is literally saying, 'Yes to God' even when we do not understand his plan and purpose, or do not even like it. It is about absolute trust in his goodness. So there it goes, after his mother's burial, they had just two weeks to plan, prepare and to do both their traditional marriage celebration and Church wedding. The wedding was on the Friday the 5th of January 1996. It was a very challenging time for both Lily and Stanley.

To begin with, two weeks was a very limited duration for all the planning, preparation and shopping. Up to the eve of the wedding, they were still shopping. Stanley spent the whole day with friends shopping for the wedding ring and other things. Lily was doing same with her family, friends and Stanley's family. The food shopping and preparation was the responsibility of the women in both families. In the evening, Stanley, Lily, the bride maids and best men had to meet in the Church for the final preparation for the wedding day. Someone reported an issue with the food preparation to Lily. She told the reporter to sort the issue out with Stanley's family who were handling that part of the food preparation. To Lily's surprise, Stanley reacted in a very insensitive way to defend his family.

The stress, the apprehension and this reaction from Stanley reactivated Lily's fears. She developed some headache and did not sleep well all night. On the wedding morning, she had pain all over her body, was very weak and unable to get out of bed. She did not feel like she could face the day. Thank God for good friends who encouraged her with their words and prayers. Three of them got into prayers around her bed. By the time they finished, her strength was restored. She was able to get up, showered and get dressed for the day, and went through it. Their support certainly saved the day. This marriage was consummated for God's glory. The devil must have been gnashing his teeth but he could do nothing about it.

Lily's awareness in this season:

- God has a plan for every detail of our lives. He wants to bless us above and beyond our wildest dream.

- Marriage is certainly very important to Him. He started it in the garden of Eden;

Genesis 2:18, 21-22; 'Then the Lord said, 'It is not good for the man to be alone. I will make a helper who is just right for him. So the Lord God caused the man to fall into a deep sleep. While the man slept, the Lord God took out one of the man's ribs and closed up the opening. Then the Lord God made a woman from the rib, and brought her to the man'. (NLT)

- God is the best match maker if we learn to listen to him and wait on him. He wants us to marry well as any good father will want for his son or daughter.

- The enemy works actively to block, confuse or distract us from connecting with the right partner as God intended.

- This is why it is very crucial to hear from God for ourselves especially before saying 'yes'. It is very necessary to learn to recognise God's voice in every area of our lives.

Jesus said, 'My sheep hear my voice…….' (John 10:27 NLT).

- Some great men and women of God can be deceived, so we

cannot rely on others to always hear for us.

- God can use others to confirm what He has already told you, not to tell you what to do.

- Having a prayer partner that we can trust is indispensable; someone we can open up to and truly share our heart in confidence. Our prayer of agreement is very powerful.

In Mathew 18:19, Jesus said, 'I also tell you this: if two of you agree here on earth concerning anything you ask, my Father in heaven will do it'. (NLT)

A combination of prayer with fasting will remove anything that the enemy has used to block us and gives us the victory. These are part of the weapons of Spiritual warfare.

The encouragement at this point to the reader is to persevere in your walk with the Lord. If you have any long standing or stubborn problem in your life or family, learn to ask the Lord for understanding, engage in fasting and prayer, and pray with trusted friends. You will surely have the victory. God meant the problems we face in this life to be stepping stones into Spiritual growth and victory. This is how God is glorified.

Even when things do not seem right, we are to have 'purpose in our suffering'. Jesus suffered with purpose because He knew the ultimate end is victory. He won the victory for us. All we have to do is to enforce it.

Isaiah 53 concluded it in verses 10 – 12:

'But it was the Lord's good plan to crush him and cause him grief. Yet when His life is made an offering for sin, he will have many descendants.

He will enjoy a long life and the Lord's good plan will prosper in his hands. When he sees all that is accomplished by his anguish, he will be satisfied.

And because of his experience, my righteous servant will make it possible for many to be counted righteous……I will give him the honours of a victorious soldier……' (NLT)

Lack of purpose in suffering releases hopelessness, anxiety and depression. This is the enemy's strategy. If you find yourself in such position, get into God's presence and press in for more of Him. Your perspective will change when you hear from Him and get to understand the purpose for whatever you are going through. We have a faithful God. He is totally and completely reliable. He cannot and will not fail us when we chose to trust Him.

Dying to our selfish desires and aspirations, and developing self-control enables understanding of the purpose in suffering.

Chapter 6

Relocating Abroad and Starting the Family

Within two weeks after their wedding, Stanley had to return abroad. He was residing in a little Mediterranean Island then. Lily was surprised to have this knotted feeling in her stomach, the dread of missing him. They really didn't have much time with each other and had no honeymoon. The two weeks post wedding was filled with one activity after the other; visiting relatives and getting things ready for his return journey. It was a wild two weeks and then off he went. This dread of missing him was also quickly replaced with the feeling of freedom after her left. The effect of his insensitive reaction on the wedding eve was that Lily never got to be herself with his family in his presence. She was on edge. But after he left, Lily was able to relax and got to know his family better and even developed a loving relationship with her father in-law, now in blessed memory. He was very fond of Lily.

Once a week, on what was called, Market day, he used to send Lily a whole bunch of green plantain through his youngest wife. He was a polygamist with three wives. It was interesting he knew what Lily liked, just like her father. This inspired Lily to visit him frequently in the village, taking him some delicacies from the town. He was an interesting and wise man. So they used to have interesting conversations. One evening, they were in his courtyard with his two wives and he said to Lily, 'I think having just one wife will be a very difficult thing for a man'. Lily responded, 'Well, Baba (that's how they all called him), if you have one thing, you would take good care of it and it will last longer for you, but having more than one means you may have the tendency to neglect or misuse some'. His wives agreed with Lily. Her father in-law just smiled and never picked on Lily anymore.

Six months after the wedding Stanley succeeded in getting her migration documents and send them to Lily. It was now her time to get ready and leave her homeland for the first time abroad. It was both exciting and challenging. The thought of meeting Stanley again and starting her family was exciting. Lily's youngest sister, Grace who has been under her care since she started work was very apprehensive of Lily leaving. As the reader, you have to understand this; there is no social services in that Country. Individuals help one another in the family. Lily's education was supported by her second brother David. When Lily became independent, he assigned Lily a responsibility and it was supporting this youngest sister, Grace. By now, Grace was in her early twenties and in the University. Lily did her best to reassure Grace that she and her husband would continue to support her. Lily had already let Stanley know about this and he had no objection. But on the day that Lily was leaving,

Grace cried so much that Lily's heart was broken. If Lily was not sure of her marriage, she would have given up. Grace was not the only one in tears, all of Lily's friends and the few family members present were in tears. Lily wept all the way to the next town where she spent a night with one of her in-laws who escorted her before travelling for several miles to where the airport was. This was the most heart wrenching separation that Lily had ever experienced in her whole life.

At the airport, Lily met with resistance. The food stuff that was prepared for her to take abroad was not allowed. She had to leave all of it with her in-law. This was very disappointing. Nevertheless, about five hours after take-off, she landed in one of the Mediterranean Country's airport. Lily had just a light cotton wear on. Stanley had told her it was very warm at this time in this country, that was in the month of June but she was shivering with the cool breeze at the airport. This was not the same as the hot and humid tropical evening that she was in five hours ago. She was also exhausted with the entire ordeal of the journey she went through for the past few days. But it was nice to see her husband again. She felt at home in the lovely two bedroom first floor flat he rented as their first home together. It was clean and tidy. Their new life began in this little village. It was a very beautiful environment, surrounded by the

Mediterranean Sea. Lily's favourite past times was strolling by the sea side in the cool of the evening enjoying the sea breeze.

There were also challenges adjusting to this new life in a strange land.

To begin with, Stanley's works rota was two long days, one night, two days off and the cycle continued. When he was off, all he wanted to do was sleep. He would wake up on his off days, have breakfast and went back to sleep. Lily did not understand how exhaustive the work was, and how his body just wanted to rest and recover before the next working days. Lily used to look forward to his off days expecting some outings and time together. Her expectations not being met, she found life boring. Stanley did not understand her either. Most of the foreign women in the Country then envied her because her husband was working and able to put bread on the table and met her basic needs whereas their husbands had no stable jobs. So Lily had no friend either who understood her. Having a relationship with God was her only source of comfort and strength.

Lily was unable to work either because the government then had shut the door of employment to foreign Nurses just before her arrival. Her life changed from being very active to virtually doing nothing, boring and unsatisfying. Stanley had money but would not buy even a Television set which could have helped her get to understand the culture. His reason was religious, and Lily hated this. This misunderstanding between them began to drift them apart. Lily felt bad she was considered very lucky whereas she lived below the standard of life abroad. Most foreign men on the Island had no stable jobs. They depended on the Catholic Churches for aid, while living as students so they could have a stay. Some did manual jobs in the farms or wash dishes in the restaurants. The women did same to survive and take care of the families. However, these people had televisions in their houses. It was all very unfair but Stanley would not give in. Lily had to learn to live with what she had and be thankful.

A friend attempted to get Lily into the job of washing dishes in a restaurant. She went once, hated it and never went back. So this life abroad was not that glamorous as some people in the developing

Countries are told. The only good thing was that Stanley did not attempt to give her this wrong impression before she came. What kept Lily going was her relationship with God. She spent most of her time in His presence, studying the Word and kept trusting Him to make a way for her. She did not want to put her nursing certificate in the box and wash dishes for a living.

And God did visit Lily. Three months after her arrival, she became pregnant with their first child. This gave her something to focus on. They were very delighted with the news. However, the first and the second trimester of the pregnancy became treacherous. What happened was that the pregnancy hormones also reactivate a dormant fibroid in Lily's uterus. The fibroid began to grow more rapidly than the baby. By the second month of the pregnancy, Lily was in constant pain, and this pain intensified so much that by the third month, she was admitted into the hospital. And she was there for the next three months because she needed regular analgesia including morphine. The obstetrician's prognosis was a miscarriage; they also were concern for her life. They advised Stanley to consent for an abortion to be done in order to preserve

Lily's life. Even some of the believers counselled Stanley to consent to it.

When Stanley told Lily, she was determined not to let a man tamper with what God has done. She just said, 'The Lord puts this baby here. He alone has the right to take it out if he wants to'. At the end, the obstetric team just decided to keep Lily under observation in the hospital. All they asked at every round was, 'Do you have any bleeding?' And her response was always, 'No'. They had resolved to carry out the abortion at the slightest sign of bleeding. This was their right for intervention out of duty of care but, thank God, it never happened.

The pain was ongoing though. One day, the pain was so intense Lily could not even get out of the bed to go to the toilet, or used the bedpan. It was not responding to the maximum dose of the prescribed analgesia either. The midwives in the antenatal ward and obstetricians did not know what to do. They could not give her any more analgesia as it would have constituted an overdose. Lily was miserable and in bed till Stanley visited in the evening. He was moved to pray and rebuke the pain. As soon as he did this, the pain lifted. Lily felt better and the first thing she needed to do desperately was go to the toilet to empty her overfilled bladder. Stanley helped her out of bed, and escorted her to the toilet. Passing urine had never felt so good because her bladder was

overstretched with urine. She felt great thereafter, walked straight back to bed and ate the food Stanley brought, her first meal of the day. The midwife thought it was her husband's presence that made all the difference. And indeed it was. Stanley later told her he was fasting and praying for the past three days, talking to God as there was no good counsel from anyone around him. He came into the ward with the fast. No wonder his prayer was that powerful. The pain never came back for the rest of the week.

The next Monday, the obstetrician decided to discharge Lily. As she was leaving the ward, he said to her, 'Please come back to the ward for admission as soon as the pain starts again'. Lily responded, 'I will be coming back for check-ups not admission because that pain will never come back. I know God touched me'. The obstetrician laughed and turns to his colleagues and said, 'Look at this woman in early pregnancy and with fibroid saying the pain will never come back'. They all shook their heads in disbelief. But it happened just as Lily said. The next time Lily went for admission was the night her labour started and by midday on the following day, their beautiful daughter came into the world. She won the battle against fibroid. Lily named her Victory. God gave Lily this name for the baby while she was still in the womb. They did not know the sex then. Stanley wanted a boy and prepared a name. It was during the labour that he suddenly catches the revelation that this is a girl, and spontaneously had another name for her. God has a sense of humour. Lily had a desire for a girl but was not particularly bothered if the outcome was a boy. She used to find it interesting when Stanley talked to the baby in the womb, he would say, 'Hey boy, be good!' And Lily would say,

'What if it is a girl?' His response was always, 'No, he's a boy'.

Nevertheless, he was happy to have a child at the end.

It was great to start a family but they also had challenges. Being new parents and many miles away from family, Stanley was a complete novice in caring for a new mother and baby. He actually got too excited and forgot Lily needed to be cared for as a new mum. He was not good with cooking and did not even like it anyway. He did not like shopping, housework and cooking because he was brought up to believe these are women's responsibilities. But he had to learn because they were abroad with no family members to spoil them with care, and it was not easy. God in His goodness sent them help. A friend's mother who visited from home came to stay with them and became their mother. She took care of Lily till she recovered from the strain of the pregnancy and labour and got back on her feet again.

This lovely woman did not stop but continued as their baby sitter because six months after delivery, the door of employment opened. The government of the land decided to register foreign Nurses especially as Enrolled Nurses. Though it was a kind of demotion, it was better than washing dishes to Lily. At last she could continue with the profession she really loved, and also supported their finances. The arrival of a baby also brought additional expenses, and Stanley's income alone was not enough to meet all their needs. So this news of employment was a very welcome opportunity. This was also additional commitment to Lily. After she started the work, this lady, who was always babysitting for them began to have some manual works as well. They began to employ the help of another relative, who was like a little sister to them, she was a student. At times, they got the help of Stanley's brother and family and other friends for childcare. Lily soon realised how unstable and risky this situation was for their little girl. Victory stopped breast-feeding at six months and preferred the bottle because mum was not always there when she needed her. One day while at work, lily's breasts were gorging. When she came home, the babysitter told her Victory cried so much that day and she struggled to comfort her. No wonder Lily felt the way she did at work that was when her baby needed her and she was not there.

It was heart breaking for Lily.

There was no sustainable child care provision in this Country because most of the women of child bearing age were not working. They were fulltime housewives and the government paid them some allowances. But to the foreigners, life was quite different; they were not even permitted to talk about child care problem at work, no flexibility allowed whatsoever. At times, Lily had to carry the baby to work and exchanged with Stanley who had finished from a long hard day. It was very stressful for all of them. They needed a change to their working condition and family life. This was the motivation for their next move.

Lily's awareness in this season:

The fact that God arranged their marriage did not mean they had an easy relationship. They actually had a lot of misunderstanding in their relationship because they did not develop friendship before the marriage.

They did not know each other's likes and dislikes and the need to meet each other's need. So in the marriage, they tend to take each other for granted. They could not communicate properly because they tend to be defensive, irritated and angry, so much hurts were not resolved but buried. Negative emotions buried alive never goes away, so these kept building up. Even in their prayers, they did not know how to be open with God and process their thoughts and emotions. This made their

relationship very unstable; loving one moment, hate and conflict the next. This is a pathetic way to relate but they thought that's how relationship is because they did not know any better. They had no good example to emulate. Unfortunately, they did not know how to get help.

The counsel to the reader is that God made this marriage relationship and sees it as good. This does not mean the absence of challenges. Actually, challenges were to be the platforms that the man and woman move into a higher level as they work together. That is why Jesus said in Mathew 18:19

'I also tell you the truth: If two of you agree here on earth concerning anything you ask, my Father in heaven will do it for you'.

A husband and wife who work together as one have tremendous power. The enemy knows this and is committed to disrupt this unity so he can steal, kill and destroy. And most times, he works through the wounds in the soul. Lily and Stanley did not know then about the wounds in their souls that gave the enemy this advantage over them. These wounds acts as landing pads for the enemy whenever they have a problem, he attacks, making it difficult for them to resolve arguments in the Spirit of love and humility. So if you are struggling continuously in your marriage or any area of your life, seek God to know what the wounds in your soul are that give the enemy the advantage over your life and relationship. Get counselling help if you need to. God wants you healed, restored and made whole so you can enjoy your life and relationship.

To the singles, the encouragement is to develop friendship before you say 'yes' even when you are aware of God's will for you. Allow God to develop that love and friendship in you for each other. Wholesome dating (getting to know each other and developing friendship without getting committed sexually before marriage) is necessary for a successful marriage. This is not old fashion. It is Godly standard.

Chapter 7

Moving to West

Stanley began to look for opportunities outside the Mediterranean Country in the sixth year of residing there. He found a hospital in the Western Nation, for Hospital orientation and subsequent registration with their Nursing Professional Body. After the brief period of orientation, he came back to Lily and daughter with some good news; he had an offer of employment. Lily was concerned about the working condition. In the Mediterranean Country, it was long days and nights, 12 hours shift pattern with nothing in between. This was not conducive for a baby as well. It was a great relief to Lily when he said there were three shifts pattern in this temperate region, which were Early, Late and Night shifts. Additional good news was availability of child care facilities and flexible shifts for parents with young children. It appeared to be just what they needed. So they decided to move to this Country that sounded like a promised land. Stanley moved down first in January to prepare the place.

On 1st April, Lily and their daughter, Victory made their way from the Mediterranean Island to the West. Lily was full of hope and expectancy. They have heard so much of how beautiful this country was. The only negative news was that it could be very cold. So, they came overdressed. Lily had to take off some of her clothes and her daughter's clothes at the airport. The sun was shining brightly like it was welcoming them into the country. It was a very lovely day. Stanley picked them up from the airport. It was nice for the family to be together again, they did miss each other.

Stanley had rented a lovely house in the doctors' quarters of the Hospital where he worked. They lived there for a while, about six months.

Lily wish they had continued to live here. Unfortunately, the unfolding story was contrary. Soon she got to know Stanley's monthly income was not enough for their rent and household bills. They had to depend on the little savings they brought from the Mediterranean. Soon this savings eventually ran out. One good thing that happened at this time was Lily having an operation to remove the fibroid at the local Hospital. The surgery went very well because the fibroid was on the outer aspect of her uterus, so her uterus was preserved. They were thankful to God for this miracle. When their savings ran out, Stanley became very anxious. He would look at their kitchen cupboards and panic. Lily tried to reassure him God would take care of them. They just had to keep on praying and trusting him.

When Lily recovered from the surgery and became stronger, she attempted to get a Care job meanwhile. She was processing her documents in preparation for registration with the Nursing Council but things did not move as fast as she had expected. She could not do many shifts either as she could not work whenever shifts were available because of her two years old daughter. These setbacks began to have a toll on them after a while. Their relationship was affected in an adverse way. Finances were the main area of the conflict as Stanley began to hide money from Lily and would not release money even for some basic needs especially for their little girl. To make ends meet, Lily began to go to Charity shops and car booth sales to get things for their daughter.

One day, at a car booth sale, she found a toy keyboard with phone in a very good condition and got it for her hoping she will play with the phone. She was very excited when she got the toy and started to play with it straight away. Lily went into the kitchen to sort out lunch. Then she heard a nursery rhyme coming into the kitchen. When she look out into the hallway where Victory was sitting playing with the toys, Lily was surprised to see this two year old playing the tune with the toy keyboard.

She was playing most of the nursery rhymes they sang together such as twinkle, twinkle little star etc. Lily just knew she was gifted. Lily shared the story with Stanley when he came back from work, and they made up their mind to help her develop this gift.

At some point, an opportunity came up for them to rent a council house which was cheaper. Lily did not particularly like the houses they were offered but at this stage Stanley did not listen anymore to her feelings and they ended up with a council maisonette. Lily soon realised it was not a good environment. They shared the building with people with all kinds of mental health problems, and people addicted to drugs and alcohol. They were the first black people in this environment. So some people were racist towards them. Being believers, they kept praying, trusting God and being kind to their neighbours. Their little girl also started in a play school in the local church they attended. It was a walkable distance from the maisonette. She loved going to this play school. She was a lively little girl, loves to have friends and to play with them. Children do not mind skin colour; they see their humanity and just love to play with each other. So life goes on.

Another venture Stanley undertook at this time with hope to make extra income to sustain the family was recording the songs he wrote I a Recording Studio located at the church which they attended. The recording went well but the CDs did not sell as he expected. The guy who did the recording for him did advise him to produce a small sample to try the market first. When he shared this with Lily, she encouraged him to listen to them. But he was so carried away with his vision and went on to produce 3000 copies. His disappointment escalated when it did not sell as he expected. This set up the stage for the devil to manipulate him. First a friend who was not a believer suggested he take the CDs to his home Country because they would sell very well there. Next his bank offered him a loan.

Lily encouraged him to pray and hear what God is saying which he did. And God did speak to him when he prayed but he did not even listened to God. He later reported after the disaster of the whole ventures that as soon as he got to pray, the scripture, 'the righteous should not borrow……..' Came into his mind. He refused to share what God was saying with Lily because he sensed she would agree with God. Lily did not actively seek God for him either because he was not listening to her.

She did think he would listen to God, that's why she encouraged him to seek God for himself.

Stanley got the loan and went off to his home Country. He lost everything, his life could have gone as well but God in his mercy preserved just his life. Stanley returned to the West with more disappointments and frustrations because now the loan has to be paid. This was additional strain to their limited income. The worst was, he did not know how to process his feelings and let go, so he became stuck. Lily did not know how to help him either. Both of them were ignorant of emotional wounds, the effects on the mind and how to get help. Their lives and relationship were not happy and fulfilling at all.

Lily's awareness in this season:

There is no perfect place on this earth. The only safe place is in the centre of God's will for our lives, and that's where our provision is. The story of Abraham in Genesis 12:1-3, became Lily's encouragement;

'The Lord said to Abram, 'Leave your native country, your relatives, and your father's family, and go to the land that I will show you. I will make you into a great nation. I will bless you and make you famous, and you will be a blessing to others. I will bless those who bless you and curse those who treat you with contempt. All the families on the earth will be blessed through you' (NLT)

Lily felt she could identify with Abram; she left her family / father's house and followed this man as her husband around. She decided to trust God to bless them and meet all their needs.

Lily was still processing her documents for registration as a Nurse in this Country. She was looking for placement in the big Hospital in the City because there were more black people there. She felt she needed black community for proper understanding and support. Lily was experiencing delays. One day during her quiet times she asked the Lord for clarity.

The Lord straightaway said to her, 'You are being rebellious also. I brought you to this community but you want to go to the City. You can fly there if you can'. Lily was taken by surprise but repented immediately and apply for placement with the local group of hospitals. Within two weeks, the process was completed and she started her Hospital placement and orientation in one of the wards that was just about ten minutes' walk from their residence. They had to pay for this placement, another financial burden. God gave her favour. She was successful at the end of 12 weeks and was offered a job by that Hospital Trust. There were a few positions to choose from. She went for night duties so she could manage her family responsibilities as well. She got the employment and commenced work in a stroke rehabilitation ward. This was 18 months after she came into the Country.

The employment brought a temporary relief to their financial struggles. Lily started work in October. By this time, she was already three months pregnant with their second child. So she was able to work for five months only before she broke off four weeks before the delivery. On Friday, 23rd of March, their son came into the world at around 4 pm. A lovely healthy baby he was. Lily named him 'God is Salvation'. Indeed her hope for deliverance and salvation from their current situation was in

God. Life in the West was not what they had expected. At the same time, Lily felt her family is complete and said to her father God, 'Thank you Lord, this is enough for me unless you have another special one you want to bring into the world through me'. And that was it. She did not have to do any family planning. Father God agreed with her, that family was complete and gave her no more babies.

The lesson Lily learned in this season is that God is with us at all times; good, bad and difficult times. We just need to keep our focus on Him and trust His leadings. But we do give in to our fears and anxieties at challenging times. That is when we take our focus off Him and try to handle our situations by our own wisdom and strength, or listen and act on the advice of others that is not according to God's wisdom. This is a terrible mistake to make because the outcome is never good. God in His mercy has provided a reset button for us in the form of repentance. Once we repent and turn back to Him, He embraces us with His love and redirects our steps into success and victory. He is a very good Father!

Chapter 8

Navigating Cultures

Navigating the Western culture was a very interesting part of Lily's experience. It all started in the first church they attended on arrival to the Island. Stanley was led to this church by the parents of his employer shortly before Lily and Victory arrived. The first day they attended the church was on Easter Sunday. Stanley was at work, so it was only Lily and her daughter who went to the church. Lily was surprised to see the setting like a party; decorated round tables with chairs around and food and drinks served. They were readily noticed and welcomed as visitors. The wife of one of the Pastors came and chatted with them. She was very warm and nice on getting to know they were Stanley's wife and daughter. She then introduced them to more members of her family. Majority of the people were white. They did feel welcome but it was not like a church service to Lily at all. The only impact she had was the testimony of the Pastor whose wife talked with them. He said in between his sermon, 'Jesus is alive! You may ask me, 'How do you know?' I know because He is in me'. This made Lily thought 'someone who is not born-again will not talk like that'. And she was encouraged to go back the next Sunday. And they continued in this church thereafter.

Then Lily noticed that women wore trousers and did not cover their heads. This was contrary to her belief then. The Bible clearly states a woman should not dress up like a man and vice versa, and also that a woman should cover her head when she prays. Lily began to wonder if these ladies were really born-again as some of them were leaders in this Church.

At some point, there was an announcement of ladies prayer meeting on a Wednesday morning that was going to be led by one of these leaders. Lily felt the Holy Spirit nudging her to attend these prayer meetings. This was easy because her daughter was now in a playgroup for two and halfhours every morning of the week day. So she had this free time. Lily would drop her daughter at the play school which was also in the same Church first floor and went downstairs to the prayer meeting. She made sure to go with her head scarf and put it on before the prayers, probably these ladies need to learn from her. Then she watched these women came in their trousers and no head scarf and they started the meeting with cups of tea first. Lily did not understand the ways of the Western ladies but during the prayers, she would feel the presence of the Lord in a very tangible way.

So again, she took her confusion to the Lord in her quiet times. The Lord just said to her, 'Go back and read what I said in that scripture'. Lily did; *'A woman must not put on men's clothing, a man must not wear women's clothing. Anyone who does this is detestable in the sight of the Lord your God' (Deuteronomy 22:5. NLT).*

And then she asked, 'Well Lord this is your word, isn't it?' He responded, 'In your culture, what is your normal dressing?' Lily knew the answer to that, they dress with wrappers. He again said, 'If a woman dresses like a man or a man dresses like a woman how would you see it?' Lily realised in her native culture people would view such a person as crazy because the way men and women tie their wrappers are significantly different. With this Lily had the understanding that men's and women's trousers were quite different. Next time she went shopping she went around looking at the differences and got her confirmation. Wow! She overcame that huddle of confusion and bias thinking with this revelation and her response to it.

Next she read about the head covering and asked the Lord for more understanding.

'But a woman dishonours her head if she prays or prophesies without a covering on her head, for this is the same as shaving her head. Yes, if she refuses to wear a head covering, she should cut off all her hair. But since it is shameful for a woman to have her hair cut or her head shaved, she should wear a covering' (1 Corinthians 11:5-6. NLT)

When she finished reading the Word, she closed her eyes and ask, 'Lord what are you saying?' And the Lord responded, 'Who is your head?' Lily acknowledged it is Stanley. He continued, 'Would he be offended if you do not cover your head?' 'Off course not, that will be ridiculous', Lily responded. Then the Lord took her back to an incident when she was in School of Nursing. The School Principal's daughter was manifesting demonic possession at home. The Principal ran to Lily's cohort as they were in the class studying. She used to call them SU (Scripture Union) people. She invited them to her home to come and pray for her daughter. They went and when they saw this girl, Lily just knew this was a case of demonic possession with manifestation. As they were about to pray, Lily suddenly realised she had no scarf on her head and pulled back. Her other colleagues tried but the prayer was not effective. They ended up referring the Principal to their Pastor. They whole family did continue in the Church after the daughter's deliverance. Here the Lord said to Lily,

'I could have used you if you had prayed without that scarf'. This revelation was so surreal. Before this incident, the principal was against them praying in the School. Lily realised the incidence was divinely orchestrated, the unbelieving Principal would have seen the power of God through these born-again praying students. A revival would have broken out in the School if she had acted by faith instead of with legalistic religious rules and regulations. After these revelations, Lily threw off her religious ways and open up to the Holy Spirit's leading. This level in her walk with the Lord was so free and refreshing.

As mentioned earlier, it was in this season that Stanley accepted the loan offered by his bank and took the CDs he recorded back home for sales. On one of these Wednesday mornings, Lily was in the prayer meeting with the ladies. The leader brought Psalm 33 for the reading. After reading, she just open the floor for the ladies to pray as lead by the Holy

Spirit. Lily felt inspired by verses 8 to 12;

'Let the whole world fear the Lord, and let everyone stand in awe of Him.

For when He spoke, the world began! It appeared at His command. The

Lord frustrates the plans of the nations and thwarts all their schemes.

But the Lord's plans stand firm forever, His intentions can never be shaken. What joy for the nation whose God is the Lord, whose people

He has chosen as His inheritance' (NLT)

Lily found herself declaring the above words and commanding frustration and destruction on the works of the enemy in their lives and families. She did not know she was praying for herself until when Stanley came back from their home Country. He told Lily he happened to get into a bus, public transport, not knowing it was operated by armed robbers in one of the major Cities in their home Country this same Wednesday morning. These armed robbers beat him up severely and robbed him of everything including his travelling passport. Their next plan was to throw him over a bridge for his dead. He suddenly opened his eyes and said, 'Please give me back my passport because my wife and daughter are still abroad and I am the only bread winner'. To his surprise, the armed robbers removed the passport from their pocket and handed it over to him. Then they dropped him by the road side. The time this happened was just when Lily made those decrees in the West with the praying ladies. God frustrated the enemies plan to destroy Stanley. He then sent his angel to get him to the nearest Hospital. From there he was able to get in contact with his cousin who assisted him till he got better. He came back to Lily with a black eye, the only evidence left from the ordeal he went through. This happened before Lily's registration and subsequent work in the West.

Victory:

This little one was twenty-two months old on her arrival in the West. She was faster than Lily in acclimatizing to the culture. Before she started play school, she was only drinking water at home, she did not like juice, squash or any sweet and sugary stuff. So the first day she started play school at two and half of age, Lily went with her water bottle and specially told the teacher to give it to her during the break. When she picked her up at the end of the day, her bottle was still full. Lily asked the teacher what happened. The teacher just said, 'Oh she saw other children drinking the squash we offered them and took to it'. And that was it. She took to everything Western including the foods like a duck to water. At the age of five, at the dinner table when their food was served she suddenly said, 'This is not the type of food people eat!' And with that she refused to eat it. Lily did not understand what she meant but her dad did and responded, 'What do you mean, we are the people. This is the type of food we eat'. For Lily, as a mum, she did not like to see her hungry, so she began to explore the Western menus and added it to their meals. Having sausages became a treat for Victory. That way Lily felt her already busy life was less stressed. She was a mum with two little children and also working full time. The work was not an easy one either. She worked night shifts caring for twenty four patients as a Registered Nurse, with only two carers in a Stroke Rehabilitation ward. God's grace on her must have been great! But on reflection later in life, Lily realised she did not know how to relax and play with her children. She was always busy and on the go.

It was later, Lily realised this little girl may have been experiencing this stress and also some racism and was trying to deal with it by denying her identity because she just wanted to blend in and be happy. One day as she was playing with a friend's son who was white in their house. Lily heard her called the boy by his name and asked, 'what is your skin colour? Mine is brown'. The boy responded, 'White'. And Victory said, 'You are pink, not white like a paper'. By now she was in reception. Lily wondered how she became aware of this differences. However, she did not dwell on it, children do say things just as they see it. Next Victory began to request to have her friends around on her birthdays. And she had quite a few friends across culture as she was a lively, playful and friendly little girl. So Lily began to celebrate her birthdays at home. Lily used the occasions to prepare varieties of their native menus and then add some of the sausages. There was an open field in front of their house where the children ran around and play after eating while the mums and or dads sat around and chat. On one occasion, one of the truly Western mum came for the first time. She was the very reserved type of a lady. When the food was displayed on the table, Lily used to make it a buffet, this dainty lady said, 'I can't eat spicy food, I don't even like the smell of curry, my husband likes it but I make him eat it only at the restaurants'. Lily did like her openness but she was not going to let it stop there because her comment made even another mum who had visited and eaten their food before to shy away. So Lily said to her, 'Why not just try it before you say no. I won't be offended if you don't like it after you have tried'. She felt encouraged and took the bait. To her surprise she liked the food she tasted. She finished a piece of chicken and went for more and enjoyed the rest of the meal. The mum who wanted to shy away overcame her fear, and everyone was happy.

Victory's birthday used to attract the rest of their neighbours, even people passing by. They would be curious about what was happening, and Lily would invite them to come in and eat with them. Through this they broke through the racism in the neighbourhood, and at the same time displayed their culture of love, openness and freedom. When they moved out of this community, Lily used to meet some of their neighbours in town and loved to chat with them, they always mentioned how they loved and missed Lily's food. It is interesting how food can break through cultural barriers and bias.

Despite all this effort to integrate with their community, there was still a residue of racism that was hard to remove. At some point, Victory started to hate going to school. Being that busy, Lily really had no time to stop and explore why. She used to come back from night duty, rushed to get Victory ready and run all the way to school which was about a quarter of a mile away. Got back home to take care of the baby and have

intermittent naps until it was time to pick her up from School again. If and when Stanley was back from work or not at work, she handed them over to him and had some proper sleep. A good sleep was all the self-care Lily needed to keep her going in this season of her life. Stanley worked all shifts so he only had to do the school runs or part of it when he was off or on late duty. Managing the family was certainly easier in the West than in Mediterranean country though. It is the demands of the work that was more stressful. Unfortunately, as the parents, Stanley and Lily were not even aware of their stress, and so did not manage it properly. This contributed to their little girl struggle in School.

To make things worse, in Year 1, Victory had a very stern Teacher. One day, as Lily went to pick her up after school, she wanted to rush out to her mum and in the process jumped the queue. The Teacher pushed her back into the class angrily. Lily went up to the Teacher and ask what the matter was. She made Lily wait until she had seen off the rest of the children and their parents. Then she called Lily into the class and told her Victory had been behaving inappropriately in class. She showed Lily a long list of all the wrong behaviour and attitudes she had displayed in class, and then asked Lily to sign the form so Victory could be sent to a School with Special needs. Lily was amazed because the behaviour she described was like that of a mentally sick person, not this little happy girl.

Lily could not understand what happened to her little girl in class. So she asked this Teacher to give her a day so she could come to the class and observe her daughter. The school did encourage parents to do this as a means of helping in the class, but Lily had no time because of work and the baby care. However, to get to the root of this problem, Lily was willing to exchange shift at work and get a baby sitter if necessary. This Teacher then said she has to discuss Lily's request with the Head Teacher before giving her the opportunity. That was fair enough, Lily did not mind waiting. After some days, this Teacher got back to inform Lily her request was not granted because they felt her daughter would be more disruptive when she sees her mum in the class. Lily sensed something not right here and refused to sign the form she wanted them to sign. Stanley was present when this Teacher gave them this outcome of their decision with the Head Teacher.

Eventually, the Head Teacher did more investigations and got to the conclusion that the way this Teacher communicated with Victory was the issue, the child does not understand her. So they got a Speech and Language therapist into the class to help. At the end of that school year, this Teacher gave Victory a very good report. This left Lily wondering what was influencing her communication with Victory before. Victory did not have this problem with any of the Teachers before or thereafter. In her year four, they had moved house and also to a different school. The first time the Speech and Language Therapist went to the new School for a session with Victory, her Teacher thought the Therapist had made a mistake because the girl had no problem. Subsequently, she was discharged from this service without any recommendations because there was no need.

Lily was convinced the Teacher who wanted to send Victory to a special school did have some kind of racism in her. Victory was the only black child in this class, and she was different in every way. This Teacher certainly had a biased mind and attitude that hindered her communication with the little girl. Had it not been that God was with them and gave Lily the wisdom to handle the situation, this Teacher would have succeeded in ruining her child's life. It was still at this time Victory

was afraid in doing maths home work. She cried whenever she had to do her maths homework, and used to keep saying, 'I'm not good with maths. Lily had to enrol her in Kumon (Private class). She began to flourish in maths so much that in the next school, she used to take part in Maths squeeze competitions. This was a confirmation that when any child is not learning, the fault is with the Teacher's or the systems. Every child wants to learn and grow. It is sad to see so many children dumped as special need children whereas each of these children can thrive and flourish if they are in a conducive environment, and with the right support. Children are great believers; they believe whatever their parents or Teachers tell them. The worst thing to tell a child is that they cannot make it because they will believe it, and this wrong belief subsequently will sabotage their lives and future. Teachers have tremendous power and influence on the children that are under their care, the outcome of their future depends a lot on this relationship.

Chapter 9

Work Experiences

Though Lily loves her work as a Nurse, she can honestly say the only season she had job satisfaction was in her home country. The highlight was in her first employment as a midwife. The independent opportunity and challenges enabled her to grow and flourish immensely in this field. By the time she went back for the double qualification training in General nursing, she did it because it was mandatory. She was very competent in taking care of the local women from pregnancy through delivery to home care and immunizations. She could handle all types of deliveries including twins and breech presentations. Once she handled competently a twins and breech delivery which the resident Doctor wanted to refer to a Specialist Hospital because she (the Doctor) could not handle it. Lily reassured the Doctor and undertook the delivery. This Doctor was so surprised and recommended Lily for promotion even before she went for her double qualification. After the double qualification training, Lily only worked for one year in a General medical / Surgical Ward as a Nursing Sister before moving abroad. This was just for experience in this area. She would have gone back to Midwifery if she did not travel abroad. Her work life in this season was purposeful, meaningful and much fulfilled.

Lily was very disappointed and frustrated in the Mediterranean Country after leaving this good work life behind. She had no purpose in doing menial/unskilled jobs so hated it. Midwifery was an area the government of this Country would not even consider a foreigner to work in. When they eventually registered Lily as an Enrolled Nurse, she felt devalued but was happy to work in this capacity just for finances. The services she offered was even better than what some of their Registered Nurses offered because she offered her best, not based on the role she was given. Her only job satisfaction was in the patients' responses, and they were always thankful. Most days, Lily returned home with boxes of presents from her patients as they expressed their gratitude to her good nursing care. The insurmountable challenge working in this Country was managing child care with the long hours of work. The constant stress was just too toxic. Moving away from it all was the best thing to do.

Working in the West had been a mixture of experiences. Lily's first employment with the local Hospital was in a Stroke Rehabilitation Ward. The Hospital was a walkable distance from their residence. It was good for the sake of managing the family as Lily had the night position that she wanted. The work itself was okay but the patient -staff ratio was not good at all; one trained nurse and two health care assistants to twenty-four dependent patients. Ninety percent of this patients needed support with their daily activities including toileting, changing of sanitary pads, and changing of positions at night. The shift used to start at 9 pm. Being the only trained to do the medication, this procedure alone could take up to 1 am because most of the patients needed to be fed with their tablets, syrups etc. Some needed medications administered via PEG (Percutaneous Endoscopic Gastrostomy) or NGT (Naso-gastric Tube). It was challenging because of the staff - patient ratio. But management never listened to staff complaints. Staff just had to get on with it.

One night duty, one HCA (Health Care Assistant) was off sick, and Lily was left with only one for the whole night. Caring for patients is hard because you just cannot ignore their needs. They were more than exhausted by the end of the shift. Lily also developed a back ache that did not resolve within her next two days off duty. She decided to go to her GP for treatment. She was diagnosed with a slipped-disc, and sent to the physiotherapist. She was also given a two weeks sick leave. After her recovery, Lily decided to look for alternative employment. By now she had worked there for longer than three years. One of her colleagues who has worked there for many years was now on involuntary early retirement because of back problem sustained on that Ward. This colleague used to complain of back pain most times but did nothing about it until one day her vertebrae just locked and she could not move. She was taken by ambulance to the nearest Orthopaedic Hospital where she underwent series of surgery. She could not recover fully and could not return to work. Lily decided to learn from this colleague's unfortunate situation. She quitted from this department while she was still on her feet and able to live normally.

Lily applied for a post in another department of the same Hospital Trust and was successful. So she started work next in a General and Vascular Surgical Ward. Lily also wanted to do days as well, not only nights, as her son was old enough to go into the nursery at this stage. There was an offer of child care in this part of the Trust with a nursery on site. The initial challenge she had was that this site was about four miles away from their home. So they needed two cars in the family. They could afford this by now and went for it. Lily started the work with some hope for a change in their life style and work balance. However, it did not all work out as planned. First, they realised the onsite nursery was a private one and the Trust did not subsidize the fees for staff as they seemed to portray in the job advertisement. Maybe Lily did not even read the small prints and did not understand the terms and condition fully. So most of her income went into nursery fees and they were left with not enough again. Besides, the days were so busy and the pay less. It made no sense to work like that. Lily needed to readjust again. She requested and was allowed to go back to permanent night duties. Their son was withdrawn from the nursery and registered in a play school which was just two and half hours a day. Lily's life returned to sometimes coming back from a busy night duty to take one child to Primary School and another to Play School. Sometimes she slept in the car for the two hours when her son was in the Play School because she was just too tired to drive back home. At times, she had a relief if Stanley was doing a late shift but he was not always able to arrange this. At some point Lily had to reduce her hours from fulltime (37.5) to part time (30 hours). A woman cannot do two full time jobs (family and profession) at the same time. As difficult as this was, because they still needed the income from her job, she had to let go of her professional progression so she could be there for my family. Doing only nights offered limited opportunity for professional aspirations in this Trust.

During this time, Lily was also fed up with living in the council maisonette. Their son was growing and becoming more active. She could not keep him inside most times in the day and let him out only when she had the time to sit and watch him play outside. She wanted a house with a private garden where her children could have the freedom to go out and play whenever they wanted. They have been waiting to be re-allocated a house by the council but it never happened. Lily talked with Stanley about this need but he did not listen to her. He could have been struggling with his own stress which he did not even know. A friend advised him to buy the council maisonette for investment purpose and he went for it. He purchased it without including Lily's name in the deed. His excuse was that Lily did not want it. This is how bad their relationship has become. Lily just said to him, 'Well, now that you have bought this for your investment, we need a house for the family'. And with this resolve, she went on house hunting.

Another event that inspired Lily's desire for a better house and living condition was bereavement. Grace, her younger sister, whom Lily had become very attached to, died suddenly in May of that year. Prior to her death, God had given her clear revelations of the spiritual situation in their family. Grace used to share the revelations with Lily and they kept praying together believing God for victory. Lily never expected the counter-attack on Grace's life to result in death. Lily was greatly shocked when she received the phone call about Grace's death from a friend and was devastated. She was not herself for months. It was so bad she could not even care for her little children. However, God came through for her. He provided help and care through Stanley, their Pastor and his wife for that season. Her prayers then were just tears. After about six months of mourning, Lily sensed the Lord encouraging her to go on holiday. That was their first family holiday. The Pastor's wife helped her in the holiday search and bookings. It was a caravan holiday in Northern part of the country. This provided Lily with an opportunity to recover. Her life perspectives changed after this. She realised how short life is and made up her mind to live well. Lily disliked the maisonette because there was no private garden for her children to play freely. She wanted a change to something better.

The first thing she became aware of after her recovery from grief however, was the deploring living condition they were living in. Their maisonette was covered with moulds. It was like 'Yuck, how could they be living like this?' She mentioned it to Stanley but his response was,

'Haven't you seen other houses worse than this?' Lily said, 'Yes, but I have also seen others better than this'. With this, she embarked on changing their living condition. She got a magazine from the nearest house decorating shop. Lily explored the painting stuff available there. They offered to pay a friend to do the painting but his price was beyond their budget. Lily decided to do it herself. She bought all the stuff and got some tips from this friend and commenced the job. The worst place was around the stairs and hallway. As Lily finished painting this part, she stopped and admired her work; the wall was immediately transformed and clean. Suddenly, she heard in her spirit, 'So you love your handwork?' She knew His voice and responded, 'Oh yes Lord! It's so beautiful'. His response surprised Lily; 'I can make you more beautiful than this', the Lord said. Lily asked, 'What do you mean?' He said no more. However, Lily had this awareness there is something not beautiful in her life and the Lord wants to work on it. So she just prayed, 'Okay

Lord, do whatever you want to do in me. I am all yours'. She never thought about this anymore. However, her desire to move into a house with a private garden intensified every day.

Lily had a little saving in her account. So she continued with the house hunting. Eventually, they found a house that they liked at Eastern part of the same town and bought it. This was in August of the following year after the new employment. They moved into their first privately own house with great excitement. They also moved the children into the nearest school which was a stone throw from their house. The children were very happy in this new house. The previous owners were so kind they left some of their daughter's toy in the garden. Lily added some more garden toys to this. Both children used to enjoy themselves there and for hours while Lily rest if she needed to without worries about their safety. Their neighbours were surprised at how close Lily's children were. Lily had been drumming into their ears that they only have each other in this big world, so they should be nice to each other. Victory did overcome her initial sibling rivalry tendencies early and became a caring older sister. This was the best house for their children. Lily wished they had continued here but they didn't. What a life!

Shortly the winter season set in. They realised the central heating described in the advertisement of the property by the estate agent was not true. There were radiators in all rooms but these were operated through a coal system. This system has been long outdated. The first time Stanley tried to put the heating on, the toxic fumes filled the whole house. Lily had to take the children out because they could not tolerate the toxic air in the house. This brought Lily and Stanley into another argument because Lily had wanted a home buyer's report done on the property before they bought it but the estate agent told Stanley he could save the money as this was a newish property. As usual Stanley listened to the estate agent rather than to Lily.

Nevertheless, he was able to hold them accountable for the problem. He wrote them a letter of complaint and followed it up till they decided to come and change the system to a modern heating system. In the process of doing this, they left part of the kitchen damaged. They could not negotiate for this to be done because Stanley cracked up with inappropriate anger and further talk was cancelled. Stanley was overwhelmed with the stress he was experiencing. They were left with this ugly section in their kitchen. Again Lily was not happy every time she looked at it. By now they could only manage to pay the mortgage monthly and had no left over income to sort out this kitchen. The property that was for investment was not rented, so they had two mortgages to pay. This was learning in a very hard way.

One day, as Lily was looking at this mess in the kitchen, a thought popped into her head, 'Re-mortgage and extend the property'. She shared it with Stanley but he just responded with, 'No, we are not borrowing any more'. However, this thought stayed in Lily's mind. So she called the bank and ask if they can lend them anymore. After some assessment, they returned to her with a positive word; they could lend them up to £15,000. Next, she called an architect and asked about the possibility of extending the house above the garage. He confirmed it was possible. She went further to call builders and asked what the extension would cost and had many quotes. Then Lily took action. She asked the bank to send the paperwork to fill for the loan, got the architect to do the drawings. She filled in all the paperwork and only asked Stanley to sign but he refused. Lily put the documents away and kept praying for God to move Stanley to sign if the project is God's will. Eventually, God did by getting a parent when Stanley went for school run to tell him how much value the extension can add to the property. He then asked Lily for the papers, signed them and Lily sent them off. Within weeks the money was released, the work commenced and by late that year, the work was completed. Their monthly mortgage payment has also increased, so their plan was to sell the property and buy a small and affordable one.

Lily underwent another adventure during this season. The following year after moving into their privately owned house, a leaflet was posted in through their door that said, 'Counselling level at the nearby College'. It was a ten weeks evening course. Lily became curios and enrolled for it.

What inspired her was that her son was diagnosed with sickle cell anaemia in his first year of life. This opened the door for her to interact with different health professionals and to receive additional help and trainings. They were referred to an organisation called OSCAR. This organisation was well funded to help the parents of children affected by this health problem. Through their support with childcare, Lily went into a free IT training course at local College for one year. Lily also met a Counsellor who suggested she could be good in counselling. This was about three years earlier but Lily did not consider it then. This time around, just seeing this information triggered her dormant desire. So she went for it. Lily took to this Course like a duck to water. She really loved it and for the first time, she began to gain some awareness of the issues in her life in relation to anger and fear. She went on to do level three. She had wanted to stop at this level but her Tutor encouraged her to go on and do the Diploma.

This Tutor was a very lovely woman. Lily could not afford do two evenings in a week due to work and the cost of babysitting. She referred Lily to another Training School that was offering one day per week part time Course. This was easy for Stanley to arrange a fix day off work to babysit. Lily only had to reduce her hours at work to only 10 so she could have the flexibility to study. At the same time, she did some agency work to supplement their income and also pay the school fees. She did not want to get a student loan. So in September the following year, Lily started a two years part time Diploma in Counselling Course. It was challenging in every aspect. The main theories were Gestalt and Person Centred. They also did the introductory on CBT, Transactional Analysis, Relationships and Solution Focused. Studying was intense.

On top of these was personal therapy, practical and group work with colleagues. Lily loved it all because she always love to study and she was having lots of self-awareness and growing though it all. She learned to be present more with her children and listened more to them. She did same with

Stanley but mostly questioned and challenged his perceptions and ways. She had become aware of how she used to just accept things without questioning him and did not want to be in that place anymore. She was aware of what she was good at, and had wanted to be herself. Of course, this did not go down well with Stanley who was so used to Lily's passivity.

He resented her new found boldness and independence.

What help sustained their marriage at this time was Lily's understanding that most of Stanley's negative thinking, attitudes and actions came from his painful childhood experiences, that he was not even aware of. And Lily felt if she is going to help people like him in the future with this skill in Counselling, she needed to start from home. That may have been one of the reason God put them together in this marriage; two wounded people to help heal one another. Except for now they were not doing that but rather wounding each other the more.

Also, as Lily underwent these trainings and personal therapy, she became aware of the things in her life that were not beautiful, and the Lord was using this training to work on her. Some of these issues were fear, distrust and anger at men, especially authority figures. Legacy of her traumatic childhood. Her coping mechanism then was desensitizing, shyness and anger. Stanley was the one who bore the brunt of her anger the most. It was not easy for him also. Walking through this self-awareness and healing was at times very painful. Their marriage almost broke at some point as Stanley was still in his painful place and cocoon in anger as well as his defensive mechanism. His anger was silent aggression. However, the Lord kept them by His grace. Lily found ways to take care of herself as she emerged fragile from her cocoon of defensiveness. At times just staying in the Lord's Presence was all she needed to renew strength.

In December of that year, they succeeded in selling their home after being in the market for almost one year. This was a breakthrough for them. In August that year, they went to a Christian Conference that was catalyst to this breakthrough. Lily had done more agency work to save money for her school fees in September. To her horror, she gave all this money as offering at this conference. She felt the Lord telling her he gave her that money as 'Seed' to sow in this conference. This was the first time she experienced this. Stanley was doing the same because he was serving at the conference and they were not always together during the offering times.

Victory actually responded for the first time to the alter call to give her life to the Lord in this conference and came back with a definite change in her attitude and behaviour. This is something Lily and Stanley should have been thankful for but they were depressed because they had no more money. When College resumed in September, they were told to pay the whole school fees at once before they start this final year. In the previous year, they paid in instalments. Why the change this year? The College authority did not give them any answer. Lily remembered standing at the queue and feeling like just leaving because she had no money and did not know what to do. Suddenly, she heard the Holy Spirit said, 'Pay with your credit card'. And that was what she did. She had never paid for anything with her credit card with the hope of paying back at the end of the month so there was no interest incurred on the payment. Now she had a huge credit card bill for the first time without knowing how she was going to pay for it. However, the house sale happened miraculously in December. This helped cleared that bill off. Lily sensed their offering at that Conference gave them this breakthrough. God works in ways they do not understand at times, but all was for their good.

The first time Lily boldly opposed Stanley was in the closure of this house sale. He wanted it to happen that December. Lily told him to let it be in January so the children can finished from the school that term, and that was to also help her tidy up her college work for the year. She also wanted them to have their Christmas in this lovely house for a proper closure. Stanley appeared to listen to her initially but after he went and informed the solicitors to close the deal in December still. Before Lily would have done nothing, but she was not going to have it this time. She just could not stand the stress this was going to cause her and the children, so she took matters into her hands, called the solicitors and told them to close the deal in January. Stanley fumed when he got to know about it and threatened to call the solicitors back to change the date. Lily stood up to him and said she will call the solicitors again if he does.

Stanley had to let go eventually but they did not communicate for days. And when the sale went through, he had all the money paid into his account. They had a joint account but he did not give this account to the solicitors. Lily resented Stanley's controlling and manipulative ways, and was mad with him for days. So what they should have celebrated become a cause for conflict, very sad indeed but that was the climax of their relationship conflict. On reflecting back at this, Lily realised she did not seek God or apply wisdom in dealing with the situation. She reacted to the situation. Not the best way to handle conflict in a relationship as this did open the door for the enemy to mess with their victory, their ability to celebrate it and move on properly.

They moved back to the maisonette in January. The community was worse than they left. Some white people and children were openly racist and even though there were more black people now, these black people children were living in fear. Victory got openly involved in fighting with the white kids in defending the black kids. Lily just felt they cannot live there anymore and began to look for another property. They found their next property in another borough. The property needed a lot of renovation work but it was more spacious and they decided to go for it.

The price was affordable as well. After completion, they had enough left over to do the renovation. It took three months to finish the work. In June that year they moved in. Prior to moving in, they had an idea of the notoriety of the place because their lovely gate was stolen. So apart from the physical work, they also had a lot of prayer warfare to engage in to change the atmosphere of this community. Lily used to go for prayer walks whenever she was not at work in the community, declaring blessings over it as the Spirit led. She also posted gospel tracts through the doors to their neighbours. Lily felt God has moved into this community through them and things had to change! 'Light be, darkness out', was her daily declaration.

Lily also felt quickened and encouraged with God's word in Isaiah 61:4

'They will rebuild the ancient ruins, repairing cities destroyed long ago. They will revive them, though they have been deserted for many generations' (NLT).

This was exactly what happened in this community by the time they moved out which was ten years after. The peace of God had reigned in this place. Some of their neighbours decided to give their lives to Jesus. Some openly confessed the place had changed for good since they moved in and were worried about the incoming buyer. The evidence also was in the house sale. It almost double the purchased price, further signifying the elevated status of this community. They did extended the house to convert it from a three bedroom semi-detached to five bedrooms. It still had a lot of space for potential improvement. The proceeds for the sale was enough to clear their mortgage and they were able to purchase another small property mortgage free.

Now back to work experience, in March when they purchased their next property, Lily had to resign from her ten hours per week contract with the Trust she was employed in for almost ten years. The staff patients' ratio here was twelve patients to one Trained Nurse, and twenty-four patients to one Health Care Assistant. The ten hours a week was more stressful than the agency shifts that Lily was doing. Her sudden resignation happened on one particular night. She had a very ill patient that was also confused. This particular patient needed a one to one care. The night co-ordinator was aware but did not care to supply the needed staff. Lily also had a dying patient who eventually passed away that night. As soon as that dying patient's body was removed, the night co-ordinator wanted to send another patient into that bed. Lily reported to her that the room needed to be cleaned and made ready before she could receive the next patient. This night co-ordinator later came around to her station just when Lily sat down to do some quick documentation for the first time since she started the shift at 19:00, this was about 01:00. She harassed Lily for sitting down and did not even listen to her. Just while she was harassing Lily the confused patient fell with all the IV connections tangled around her. The night co-ordinator then left to help sort out the bed. It was like being in a nightmare. Lily put in her resignation the following day. She felt she was better off working as an agency staff. After all she could make as much income as she wanted and without the stress. Lily actually got to enjoy nursing work again as an agency staff. She just focused on the patient's care without being entangled with the ward / hospital bureaucracy. By this time, she was working with two Nursing Agencies.

Lily completed her counselling Diploma in two years. Prior to completion, she had found a student placement with one of the prominent

Counselling Centres in the big City at the beginning of the final year. Lily carried on with the placement through another year after completing her required hours. This was a voluntary work for the Organisation. Lily could have continued with them and work towards her accreditation but they decided to employ some CBT Counsellors according to the government policy then. Lily felt not needed and decided to move on. In January after ending the volunteer work, Lily networked with a group of Counsellors in the City and started her private Counselling business. Lily was excited with this new venture, and this is still ongoing though it has gone through many twists and turns including name changed and location.

Lily's next employment was two years after the above resignation with a private company specialising in homecare. Her role was nursing care for Mabel, a 21 year old young woman with complex health needs. Mabel's history was that of complications from brain tumour surgery at the age of 12 years. Prior to this she was diagnosed with Diabetes Insipidus. By the time Lily met her, she had loads of complications which were:

- Stroke with right sided weakness

- Diabetes Mellitus

- Deep Venous Thrombosis and Pulmonary Embolism

- Hydrocephalus: water in her brain. She had a ventriculo-peritoneal shunt to divert fluid from her brain into her abdomen. Blockage of this will cause her to have seizures. Later she was diagnosed with Epilepsy.

- Severe post-operative neurological deficits: speech problems, mobility problems so she was wheelchair bound

- Reduced bone density

- Hormonal deficiencies

- Cognitive and behavioural problems

- She was doubly incontinent

- She had a PEG (tube from abdomen into her stomach) for fluid, and a permanent Supra-pubic catheter for draining her urine.

Mabel needed a Trained Nurse and a health care assistant to care for her 24 hours because of her complex medical and nursing care needs. She needed vigilant and constant monitoring of her fluid intake and output as she had electrolyte imbalances at an ongoing basis. She also needed daily blood samples taken for glucose level monitoring and for Warfarin prescriptions. She had total dependence on the staff for all activities of daily living. She had challenging behaviour as well. She was capable of turning aggressive and scratching the staff with her only functional hand in a very bad way. Sometimes the strength she had at these times could take more than two staff to care for her.

The first time Lily met Mabel was during her admission at the local Rehabilitation Hospital. The newly employed staff needed some trainings with the nursing staff and the team of experts who were involved with her case. The company that employed the new staff and her parents were present in the training room also. Lily's heart went out to Mabel's mother, Jane as she described her daughter's condition and care. Her dad, Easton was very quiet, he said very little during the meeting. Mabel had an older sister who was married and two nieces who were not present in the initial meeting. After this meeting, the new staff all went to be introduced to Mabel in the ward. Just seeing this young woman so afflicted caused a well of compassion to fill Lily's heart for her. From Lily's personal experience, she knows some illnesses are beyond medical interventions and only God can resolve it. Straightaway, Lily began to felt maybe she was there to bring that awareness to this poor mother, Jane and her family. Lily kept this thought to herself initially and prayed for wisdom.

Lily's first shift with Mabel was on the 7th of June at the Hospital. It was a night duty. This was arranged so the new staff had on hand training with the ward staff in caring for Mabel, understanding her and her complex needs. At some point in the night, Mabel complained of pain on her left leg. Her medications were kept by the ward staff. Lily went to the staff to request for pain relief for her. The staff on duty was busy with another patient and promised to come as soon as she was ready. Lily went back to Mabel to see her more agitated and restless with the pain. Lily offered to pray for her and she nodded her head in consent. So Lily just put her hand on Mabel's leg and rebuked the pain. Instantly, Mabel settled back and slept being pain free. By the time the staff came over, Mabel did not need the pain relieved anymore. During Lily's break that night, she dropped off to sleep in the chair she was sitting on and had a dream in which she saw someone with jelly like stuff coming out of the leg. When she woke up, she had the impression this was about Mabel and the pain in her leg was not just ordinary pain. This confirmed her initial perception that the enemy was at work here. The outcome of this encounter was that Mabel warms towards Lily. She began to trust Lily and was not aggressive when Lily was part of the team giving her personal care. This relationship went so well that Lily could even take Mabel's blood samples on her own. Other staff could not do this, they always needed the assistance of the health care assistant The mum, Jane was really surprised at this. Lily used the opportunity to tell Jane God can help her by healing her daughter. She went on to give Jane a book that people gave testimonies about their miracles to Jane with the hope to encourage her. Jane appeared pleased initially with Lily.

Mabel stayed in the hospital till their home was adapted and the new staff were all signed off as competent in her care. Eventually, the day came when she was discharged home. Lily's hours with her were 36 per week and night duties. Prior to this time, Lily had series of strange dreams and physical encounters with Jane, the mum that she did not understand. At times, Jane would come into the ward at unusual times in the night and make unnecessary demands. Lily used to think she was just a worried and anxious mum, and tried as much as she could to pacify her. And because Lily felt for her as a mum, she used to encourage her to call on God for help. When Mabel was discharged home and after a while,

Jane's true colours began to show. More about this later. Lily was in this employment for two years.

After this employment, Lily was just happy to work agency shifts as a Nurse and practised Counselling part time and privately. She did work briefly in a Nursing Home but soon realised the job was not right for her. Lily had to give this employment up after three months, she just could not do it.

At the age of 53, the Lord used one of the members of her Church, to encourage her. Lily applied for a very unusual work that enabled her to use her counselling skills and spiritual experiences to help people. Although the pay for this job was half of what Lily used to earn, the opportunity to guide people to her Lord and Saviour made the job more purposeful and fulfilling. Lily's passion is to make Jesus Christ of Nazareth known.

Chapter 10

Spiritual Experiences

In her home country, Lily could not differentiate her religious experiences with spiritual experiences; both were merged as one, especially when she became born-again. Going to church in her country was actually fashionable. Other practices such as traditional worship or visit to witch doctors there is clearly seen and recognized as devilish and evil, therefore avoided by some church goers. Unfortunately, the devil has also disguised himself as an angel of light and deceived a lot of people to worship him in the form of a church; such was the case with Lily's father. Her father would not go to a witch doctor but did not know he was practicing the same thing in the form of a church. This is the worst kind of deception. Many people in the West think witchcraft is only in Africa because they can see these practices clearly with their physical eyes. However, this is not true. The truth is, it is hidden in the West. How can you recognize a witch in the West? One can only recognize this with spiritual insight. Sometimes those who practice witchcraft in the West appear to be the nicest people in the natural. But don't be deceived, their kindness is not without a cost to the one receiving.

In the Mediterranean, Lily recognized the atmosphere is mostly religious but most of these religious practices are based in negative spirituality which is still deception. The dominant church in this small Mediterranean Country is nothing but sheer idolatry. Some people claimed to get to know Jesus in these Churches. Lily believed at times Jesus just breakthrough this in order to reach the people he wants to draw to Himself in the only way they could understand. And because of the idolatrous stronghold in this nation, the few true churches are struggling. Much prayer is needed for a breakthrough revival. This will surely happen before Jesus comes back.

It was in the West that Lily heard people say things like,

'I am not religious but spiritual'.

This got her thinking about what they mean because when she ask, they could not explain. But thank God who opened her understanding.

One summer evening, Lily was walking to work at her first place of work. She was admiring the neatly mowed and designed lawns and houses in her neighbourhood, and at the same time wondering how the people in this country got to create such beautiful environments. Suddenly, God's voice jolted her out her of thoughts. She heard clearly inside of her, 'Do not admire the physical beauty of this place because it is very dark spiritually'. Lily was shocked but heard no more. As she continued to reflect on these words, she felt the Lord asking her to start a ladies prayer meeting to pray for leaders beginning with the family, church, religious organizations, communities and nations. By this time, they had moved from the local church they joined on their arrival to the country to another church. This church branch was started by one of their friends. She did share her vision with them and they felt it was just right to support her. The pastor was sent from their home Country and lodged with Lily and Stanley. Lily was a busy mum working 30 hours a week, and did not think she could handle any more responsibility. However, God made a way for Lily to respond in obedience to his leading. Lily felt like and shared her conviction with the pastor's wife was based in another City. She immediately felt the same, and then gave her an idea on how they could do it. So they began to wait on the Lord one day a week with fasting and pray remotely, and at times pray on the phone if they have an urgent issue that they needed to share. They recruited other ladies in the church into this prayer meetings. God released his grace upon their lives and families.

Lily began to experience shifting atmospheres, lots of revelations, informed by dreams of events even before the occurred. It amazed her that as they prayed, God began to deal with issues that affected their lives and families as well. On the 15th of January, Lily had a dream in the night. In her dream, she saw people blindfolded and locked-up in huge vessels. They were still alive but did not even call for help. The people who locked them up were living all around Lily. As Lily was looking around these vessels, these people were spying on her quite aware that she knew what was going on. Lily ignored them and kept exploring the environment. Then she saw a little child in one of the vessels. She got angry in the spirit and said, 'How dare they also lock up an innocent child? These adults locked up might have been guilty of one thing or another'. Then Lily reached out without knowing how and got this child out of the vessel. When she turned around, her sister in-law was standing beside her. Her sister in-law said, 'These people have seen what you are doing and they will attack you later'. Lily responded, 'I have a God who can protect me, so I am not scared'. Next, Lily went with this child into her sister in-law's house. The dream ended and she woke up.

Lily did not understand the above dream until on the 10th of February of the same year. This is what happened: Grace called Lily on the phone at about 10 pm. She said a great revelation had happened at home; their step-brother's children were confessing of getting involved in witchcraft. They confessed their grandmother; Lily's father's first wife was the one who initiated them into it. They also mentioned other family members who were involved in this practice. Lily was not surprised about the adults' involvement but that of the children was indeed a surprise. She then understood the child she rescued in her dream was one of this stepbrother's children. The unfortunate thing about the situation was that this step-brother and wife were born-again Christians. How did that happened to their children? Christian parents need to be awake spiritually and watch over their household. The good news was that they were able to get their children delivered. Lily seized the opportunity to recruit her sister and sister-in-law into the remote prayer regiment. There is no distant with prayers. At last the secret code of her father's church had been cracked. It was a witchcraft organisation in the name of a church. People need to know what they worship.

Then disaster struck on the 27th of May at exactly 17.45 pm, Lily received a phone call from her secondary school friend. She told Lily Grace died on the 21st of May. Lily was devastated with shock. 'How did that get to happen?' Grace had been reporting some illnesses to Lily. Lily just kept praying for and encouraging her to stay strong. God has been using her to expose this witchcraft network in the family, so an attack from the devil was not a surprise but Lily had confident God was able to protect her. To hear she was dead was devastating. Lily cried out to God for answers. There were series of dreams Lily had in this season that she did not understand but as she wept in the Lord's presence, He began to bring them back into her mind. He reminded Lily, He was trying to tell her what was going on but Lily was too busy and not really listening. In one of the dreams, it was Lily's step-sister who introduced her husband to Lily. Lily looked at the man and sensed he was not from God. She challenged her step-sister as to why she could say 'yes' to such a man in the man's absent. As she did this, the man came back. Lily pushed her step-sister into a house and shut the door against the man. Then she turned and faced him and said, 'Now you cannot have her anymore'. Lily woke up at this stage. The Lord now explained to Lily the biggest mistake that Grace made. She was 30 years old and still single. She desperately wanted to get married. The devil sent his agent to her. Because of her desperation she did not seek God for clarity. She gave herself away. The Lord used Lily's prayers to take her home. She was a wounded soldier. Her dead did leave Lily broken for some months.

Another dream the Lord brought into Lily's awareness during the grieving season, and that helped comforted her was a dream she had on the 3rd of May, the month Grace died. In this dream, Lily saw herself living in an environment that was so dark that she could not even see the people around her, but was hearing their voices. Lily was also going down a road that was very rocky. There were signposts on either sides of the road warning people not to turn into any of the side roads as all were dangerous. Somehow, as she was going up the road, she could hear a man's voice telling her to hold his hand so he could guide her but she would not, because she could not see his face and could not trust any voice. As she travelled along, there came a glimpse of light at the end and Lily was able to see this man's face. He said to her, 'I was the one telling you to hold my hand…' Lily woke up before she could respond to him. In her grief, the Lord reminded her of this dream and revealed to her that it was about Grace, not her. In Grace's distress and confusion, towards the end of her life, Jesus was there encouraging her on the journey through the valley of the shadow of death. And at the end, he received her into glory. The knowledge that the Lord received her brought all the comfort and peace that Lily needed into her soul. Her life was never the same after that bereavement period.

In December of that same year, Lily's son was very ill and admitted at the Children's Hospital for 14 days. He was only three years old then. So, Lily took time off work and spent it in the hospital with him. Her baby was unconscious for days. Lily spent her days and nights in fasting and prayers until her baby regained consciousness. She did sense in her spirit that the enemy was attacking her child and she had to fight in God's presence. On the night of the 22rd of December, Lily had a very vivid dream in the hospital. In her dream, the sayings of her late father kept coming to her as a report many times. He used to say most times, 'If those in the heavens let me, I will do this or that….' Lily woke up baffled and wondered why she was dreaming about that. In her quiet time with the Lord, she inquired but had no clarity. So she just went about with the hospital routines. By this time her baby had improved so much that when the Doctors came on Ward Round, he was doing some gymnastics on his bed, completely back to his happy energetic self. The Doctors were surprised at his sudden improvement but Lily was not. She knew it was a miracle. They planned to keep him for observation one more night. After the Doctors round, Lily got him out to the play room. As she sat down and played with him, the dream flooded back into her mind. She heard the Lord said into her spirit, 'Do you know what your father used to refer to as 'those in the heavens?' Lily responded, 'No'. Then the Lord went on, 'That was the power of witchcraft. It ruled your father's life and it is what rules in this country'. Lily was surprised at the revelation. Then she asked the Lord, 'What has that got to do with me, why do I dream about this?' The Lord said, 'Because I want you to pray for that power to be broken'. Lily asked, 'How?' But she heard no more. Lily reflected on this revelation all day. The Lord opened her understanding more to what being spiritual but not religious means in the West. The next day, the 23rd of December, her son was discharged from the hospital. Lily went immediately to the City's Shopping Centre and did her Christmas shopping. They had a big celebration on the Christmas Day to the glory of God. Shame to the devil, he lost the battle again.

On the 2nd of January the following year, a 49-day fasting and prayer commenced in their church then. The Lord had already impressed on Lily to join the fast when it was announced at the end of the previous year, so she responded in obedience. It was challenging rushing around with work and family responsibilities but God's grace was sufficient. One day Lily was very exhausted as she came back from work to prepare her 8 years old daughter and 3 years old son, dropped her daughter in her school and took her son to his playgroup. Then within two and half hours having to pick up her son, and returned for her daughter. At her daughter's School gate, Lily could not get out of the car because she was so exhausted. She put down her head on the steering wheel of the car and just said, 'Lord please help me'. Immediately, she felt a surge of supernatural strength from her inside out, her whole body came alert. Lily got out of the car, and got her baby out and they went and collected her girl. She went home and continued with the rest of her responsibilities for the day. God indeed was her strength as confirmed in this scripture;

'God is our refuge and strength, always ready to help in times of trouble'

Psalm 46:1 (NLT)

After this fast, the first significant thing that happened was God uprooting the chief witch in their family who recruited others into it, her father's first wife. Lily was actually praying for her repentance and salvation but she did not witness it on this side of eternity. Lily knew much prayer was still needed anyway for the deliverance and salvation of the rest of her family members. She could only do her part, which was to pray. She believed God would answer her prayers and in His own way and timing.

In the coming year, Lily had another Spiritual encounter. They were living then in their first privately owned property. Lily was doing Level 3 Counselling Theory and Practice at the local College. She had a classmate by the name of Eunice. In a class session where they did dream interpretation, Eunice shared a dream of seeing herself eaten up by the insects call ladybirds. Lily did not know much about dream interpretation in this way but felt it was not a good dream. She began to feel some compassion towards Eunice and started to pray for her in her quiet times with the Lord. A few weeks after, their tutor said Eunice had something to share with the class as she would not be able to continue in the training with them. To their surprise, Eunice shared she has been diagnosed with terminal cancer and has been given a few months to live. She could not continue in the training because of that. She was only 38 years old. During break time, Lily wanted to talk with her. She consented and went outside with Lily. Lily began by telling her God loved her and could heal her. She asked Lily about how she got to know God. Lily shared her testimonies of salvation and healing with her, hoping to encourage her. Eunice listened and at the end just thanked her. They went back into the class at the end of the break period. Eunice did not come back to class after that but Lily had so much burden in her heart for Eunice and kept praying for her. One day, Lily felt like writing her a letter to re-emphasize her verbal discussion about God's love for her and His desire to help her. Lily took this letter into the next class. Her intention was to give it to one of Eunice's friends to deliver to her. To Lily's surprise this friend refused to deliver the letter saying Eunice does not respond to her calls or visits, so she has not been seeing her. Lily felt so sad about it because at this stage Lily felt Eunice needed her friends more. To be isolated when in such a difficult time is the worst thing that can ever happen to anyone. One of their colleagues saw Lily's predicament and offer to help. Her name was Gina. She said to Lily, 'I can take you to Eunice after class because I know where she lives'. Lily said to her, 'No, I would not like to go to her without her invitation'. But Gina persisted saying she would never invite anyone, she just went there to see and help her. At times Eunice opened the door for her but sometimes she would not. Lily was convinced and thought even if she would not open her door for them, she could post the letter through the door to her. And so after class, they went to Eunice house.

Eunice did opened her door to them. It was appalling to see how much she had deteriorated. She was all alone in this three bedroom semidetached house. She was too ill to go up the stairs for elimination, so she kept a bucket downstairs for that. Gina has been going in to help her clean up and made her meals. Lily was speechless seeing her like that. Gina pleaded with her to come and stay in her house but she refused. Lily's voice became loosed at this point and she said to her, 'You know what? Eunice, we are just trying to help you but if you keep refusing help, there is nothing that we can do'. When Lily said that, Gina decided to go and empty her bucket saying to her, 'Lily, it seems you can talk better with her'. When Gina left, Eunice said to Lily, 'I feel I will die in this house tonight'. Lily responded, 'Is that what you want?' She responded, 'No'. Lily said, 'Then come out with us, at least if the worst happens, Gina can call ambulance for you'. Eunice then consented and brought out her key that was in her pocket. Prior to this she was telling them she could not find her key. Lily took both of them in her car to Gina's house that night.

The next morning, Gina called and asked if Lily could take care of Eunice for a few hours as she had an appointment to attend to. Lily happily consented, went to Gina's house and brought Eunice to hers. Eunice was so ill now that Lily had to assist her up the stairs to their bedroom. She left Eunice in their bed to rest as she could not even sit up. When she came downstairs, she felt this awesome burden to pray. Lily went on her knees by her dinning chair and prayed in tongues for a while until she felt a relief. The Holy Spirit just took over her because she did not even know what she was praying. At the end she just had the feeling to go and talk with Eunice. She went up to the bedroom. Eunice was awake. Lily offered her something to eat but she refused saying she was not hungry. Lily then began the conversation:

Lily: Eunice, do you know God loves you and only wants to help you?

Eunice: 'No, I don't want to have anything to do with God'

Lily: 'When you think about God, what comes to your mind?'

Eunice: 'God! Isn't he so powerful?'

Lily: 'You are right. God is very powerful but you know what, He does not abuse His power. He can only tell you He loves you and wants to help you. But He cannot force you to accept His love or help'.

The conversation ended there. However, Lily had an awareness Eunice has had an encounter with God at some point in her life or else she would not know God is very powerful. Lily did not feel the need to explore this with her. She felt all Eunice needed to know for this season was that this all-powerful God loves and cares about her. Soon after this conversation, Gina called and requested Lily returned Eunice to her. And Lily did.

The following morning, Gina called Lily saying, 'Come and see what your prayers has done'. Lily was free, so she went. To her greatest surprise, Eunice was up and standing by herself. Tears were continually flowing in her eyes, tears of joy that she could not stop. It turned out that during the night; she had eventually decided to open her heart to the Lord Jesus. And the Lord met with her. She was saved, healed, delivered, restored and made whole. How awesome and good our God is! What a great demonstration of His love, power and glory in a single night. Lily was amazed and thankful to the Lord. Eunice became a transformed person and started to go to church with them. The first Sunday she went to church with them was the 9th of July.

The joy of the Lord was radiating from her soul and her physical appearance was so beautiful. She then began to open up to Lily about her past life where she was involved in all kinds of occultism, eastern religion, alcohol addiction and homosexual lifestyle. Now she was so thankful to Jesus for saving and keeping her alive. She wanted to be part of the church family and enlisted in some programmes in the church. It was here that she met with some disappointments though, and withdrew. However, she did know the difference between Jesus and the church, the church is full of imperfect people but Jesus is perfect and faithful.

Eunice's deliverance did also open up other issues with Gina. The following week after Eunice's miracle and after class, Gina said to Lily, 'I do not understand it. I was also trying to help Eunice with herbs and my crystal ball readings but it did not work'. Lily now had a clear understanding of what was going on and said to her, 'Gina that is a wrong power (witchcraft power) that you are trying to use. If you want true power, turn to Jesus'. She was really puzzled but she decided she wanted Jesus in her life and allowed Lily to pray with her. She even went to some conferences with Lily's family. Lily gave her a book to read after that to help her in her growth as a believer. Gina accepted it but she did not fully yield to Jesus. One day, she brought the book back to Lily and said, 'Jesus does not work for me'. Lily said to her, 'No Gina, there is no disappointment in Jesus; the issue is on your side'. She declined any further discussion and just left.

After this encounter, Lily began to have series of dreams that she was being attack and Eunice was being pursued but the clarity of the pursuer or attacker was not clear. Lily just keep praying about it. At some point, Lily felt like writing Gina a letter to address what she said to her verbally. Lily explained in her letter that as she alone had the choice to open the curtain of her house at the break of day to let in the sunshine or leave the curtain on and stay in the dark all day, so it is in relating to Jesus. She is the only one who can open the curtain of her heart to let Jesus in or chose to keep the curtain, keep Jesus out and stay in the dark'. Lily posted this letter through Gina's door as she had avoided Lily during these times. Then one day, Gina suddenly knocked on Lily's door. She came in with a box of pizza saying she took it to Eunice but Eunice has decided to avoid her and not let Gina into her life anymore. The dreams of attacks that Lily had been having flooded into her memory. Lily just said to her, 'Why don't you leave Eunice alone? She is an adult and can take care of herself'. She offered the pizza to Lily but she refused it with a 'No, thank you. We have had our dinner'. Suddenly, Lily's little boy who was playing around ran to her crying of pain. Lily was angry in her spirit as she hug her son and rebuke the pain in anger. Lily's son was free and went back to play. Gina left immediately. Lily realized that was an encounter with witchcraft power through this this friend, Gina.

The next time she saw Gina was in a shopping centre almost a year later. She told Lily she was angry with her when she received her letter, but it was later she realised Lily was right. Whatever she did thereafter, she did not tell Lily and Lily did not bother to know either. It was up to her.

Meanwhile, Eunice went into hiding because of all those negative experiences in the church and the attacks from Gina. One thing Lily had confident in was that Eunice will cling to Jesus because she has experienced His awesome love and goodness, and Jesus will keep her safe. Lily can identify with this in her own faith journey.

In John 10:27 - 30, Jesus said, 'My sheep listen to my voice; I know them, and they follow me. I give them eternal life, and they will never perish. No one can snatch them away from me, for my Father has given them to me, and He is more powerful than anyone else. No one can snatch them from the Father's hand. The Father and I are one'.

So Lily had confidence in Jesus' ability to look after Eunice and did not worry about her.

Here is Lily's next Spiritual adventure:

'I will give you the treasures of darkness, riches stored in secret places, so that you may know that I am the Lord, the God of Israel, who summons you by name' (Isaiah 45:3 NLT)

This scripture came alive in Lily's heart with this next Spiritual encounter though she had struggled to really understand it. However, she chose to believe and receive. Lily was working then in Homecare with Mabel, a young adult with complex medical need and challenging behaviour in this season. As mentioned in the previous chapter, Lily developed much love and compassion for this young woman because of her situation and for the mother because she also was a mum who had experienced the distress when her child was ill. So she tried her best to help them. However, when Mabel was discharged home from the Hospital, the Homecare staff had to work with her from there. Things went on well for the first couple of months at home. Mabel was improving and flourishing with their care. She was enrolled in an art school to help improve her living standard. Lily recalled now how happy she was when she went to work one day and greeted her with, 'Hello Mabel, how are you today?'

And she responded cheerfully, 'Fine'. Everyone in the house was surprised because she has never spoken so clearly before then. Her Mum used to say that she could talk but just refused to. Lily was not surprised because this young woman had gone through so much trauma from the age of 12. Trauma shuts the sufferer down.

After a while, the staff began to see another character in her mum, Jane. She was manipulative and controlling. She wanted to control every care that was given to Mabel even against Carers' professional expertise. Mabel's aggressive attitude became worse as well. She scratched most of the staff terribly during care. Staff were full of bruises because of this. Lily was the only one not scratched until much later. On October 31st that year, mum made a vampire custom for Mabel and prepared her for Halloween party. Lily was surprised and asked her why she made a vampire custom for her daughter and why she was involved in the Halloween celebration. Once she showed Lily a cross necklace on her neck claiming she was a Christian. Jane responded to Lily's question this night by saying it was just a harmless and fun celebration started by a particular group of people. Lily refuted her saying it was not harmless and that there was no fun in Halloween celebration. Her husband who was listening to this conversation quickly went into the Internet to research about Halloween. He communicated his findings to confirm what Lily was saying. The conversation ended there.

Lily was left with this uncomfortable feeling about Jane. It was either she was an ignorant Christian who has sold her soul and family to the devil or she actually knew what she is doing, indulging in wickedness. Lily had also been having conflicting dreams about her. One clear dream was seeing her operating a shop where she was buying and selling. Mabel was with her in the shop. As Lily passed by, Mabel secretly waved at her. When Lily woke up from that dream, she just had a sense

Jane was into something evil and was using her daughter as scape goat. But she kept this thoughts to herself and in prayers.

This 31st of October was a Monday. Lily used to work nights with Mabel on Sunday, Monday and Tuesday. So this Halloween party night was during her shift. Lily made the family aware she would not take Mabel to the Halloween party. However, there was another staff that was willing to do Lily's shift. Lily happily let her, and took a leave. The report Lily had later was that Mabel levels of scratching staff escalated that very night after the party. That was when it happened to Lily on her next shift. Mabel gave Lily a very big scratch on her right arm. And she did it in a very subtle way. She was not struggling during the personal care that morning at all with them. Lily only noticed the scar when she went to wash up her hands. Lily was very surprised and on handing over warned the day staff, Trudy, who took over from her to be more careful. Lily went home and rested after the night duty.

When she woke up, she had her quiet time with the Lord as usual. She was grieved by the scar from Mabel's scratch and took it to the Lord in prayer. Lily said to the Lord, 'you cannot give me a job that I will end up full of scars, this is not a blessing and I need your intervention'. Lily heard nothing until after she read the scripture of the day which was Psalm 29 from Inspiration Reading Guide:

'Honour the Lord, you heavenly beings; honour the Lord for His glory and strength.

Honour the Lord for the glory of his name. Worship the Lord in the splendour of his holiness.

The voice of the Lord echoes above the sea. The Lord of glory thunders.

The Lord thunders over the mighty sea.

The voice of the Lord is powerful; the voice of the Lord is majestic.

The voice of the Lord splits the mighty cedars; the Lord shatters the cedars of Lebanon.

He makes Lebanon Mountains skip like a calf; He made Mount Hermon leap like a young wild ox.

The voice of the Lord strikes with bolts of lightning.

The voice of the Lord makes the barren wilderness quake; the Lord shakes the wilderness of Kadesh.

The voice of the Lord twists mighty oaks and strips the forests bare. In His Temple everyone shouts, 'Glory'.

The Lord rules over the floodwaters. The Lord reigns as King forever.

The Lord gives his people strength. The Lord blesses them with peace'. (NLT)

When she finished reading the above, she shut her eyes to meditate on what the Lord is saying. Clearly His voice boomed in her spirit, 'Do you know whose voice is the voice of the Lord'. Lily responded, 'Of course Lord, it is your voice'. He responded to Lily's surprise, 'No, it is your voice when you say what I want you to say'. This revelation was awesome to Lily. She became aware there is something the Lord wanted her to say, so she asked, 'What do you want me to say, Lord'. He responded, 'Decree that Mabel will not scratch the staff anymore'. And Lily obeyed sitting up there on her bed, 'Mabel, in the name of Jesus, I decree you would not scratch the staff working with you anymore'. Then she worshipped the Lord and finished with her quiet time. She went on to care for her family before going back to work that night.

When Lily arrived at the house and during taking over, Trudy, the staff she handed over to in the morning reported that Jane, Mabel's mum was very happy when she heard Mabel had scratched Lily in the morning. Jane overheard as Lily handed over to Trudy in the kitchen, she was sitting in the lounge. Trudy said as she came out from the kitchen into the lounge, she saw Jane smiling with satisfaction. For the first time Lily became fully aware of the evil operating in that household. Lily made further decree that her blood would turn bitter in Jane's mouth. Lily further realised the nature of her assignment in this job which she was not aware of at the beginning. The Lord wanted to encounter the forces of wickedness in the heavenly realm through her. He had been giving her series of dreams for this revelation but Lily was too religious trying to preach to this wicked lady to really understand and allow the Holy Spirit to lead her. Lily remembers once reading Mathew 10 and verse 16 leapt at her;

'Look, I am sending you out as sheep among wolves. So be wise as snakes and harmless as doves'.

In her spirit Lily heard, 'I am sending you as a lamb among a pack of wolves but remember me and you are intimately connected. Just stay there and pray but don't attract attention to yourself'.

Lily now began to understand there was more to this job than the physical nursing care. Allowing Lily to be scratched further opened Lily's spiritual insight and understanding. Lily further realised she was there to watch over the rest of the staff as well. One health care assistant used to say she loved to work with Lily because the atmosphere was always different when Lily was there. The puzzle began to fit in and Lily came awake and more alert.

The Lord established the decrees that Lily made. Mabel was unable to scratch the staff from then on. She literally just lost the power to scratch. It was interesting to see that what was attributed to behavioural problem was actually spiritual. Jane became berserk. She was angry, verbally aggressive and abusive to the staff and lied about their care constantly. Meanwhile, she avoided Lily. She stayed all day aggravating the day staff until it was close to Lily's time of duty, then she left just before Lily arrived. That was okay with Lily because they then had the peace to care for this poor, battered and bruised physically and spiritually young adult. The glaring revelation Lily had was that Mabel was being used as a human sacrifice on the altar of witchcraft. The mother was just part of it. It was a long standing worship in the family. Lily used to find herself praying through her shift and most times in tongues. She was also becoming aware of the attacks on her and her family especially on her marriage. Lily just stayed in the place of prayer and kept going. She knew the battle was the Lord's and He has never loss in any battle. God was faithful in keeping and protecting her and her family.

A significant event happened on the night of 7th February to confirm above revelation. This night Mabel was returning home after two weeks admission in the Hospital where she was treated for constipation. Jane, was manipulating and controlling staff and her care. She did not allow staff to give her the prescribed laxative when they observed her daughter was having constipation initially. Staff even called the doctor to review her. To their surprise, the doctor agreed with Jane. So no laxative was given to this poor girl until she became ill with faecal impaction and needed hospitalization. On this eventful night, mum and dad came to help staff settle her. A very welcome gesture you would think, but they obviously had their reason. Mabel was calmly sitting on her wheelchair until mum arrived and started to wheel her into her room. She became agitated and did not want to go in there. Mum had taken time to decorate the room with all kinds of fairy images. When she mentioned this, Mabel became even more agitated and started to fight and actually scratched her. Lily noticed she was afraid of something and just kept reassuring her in a calm voice. Mum left as soon as Mabel was in bed without even saying any further word to them. She acted in a very unusual manner. All along Lily was praying in her heart because spiritually she could sense another presence. A song popped up in Lily's heart, 'All other gods, they are the works of men. You are the only God, there is none like you'. Lily prayed, read the scriptures and sang this all night, and spent the night in the room with Mabel. She only left her when she was on break because the carer then took over. There was great peace in the house. Mabel at times opened her eyes and looked at all those images of fairies and queen of heaven, and went back to sleep peacefully. The enemy could not hurt her or the staff on duty because of the Lord's Presence. God showed up and displayed his power in an immense and awesome way.

The next day, 8th of February, Lily was back at work. During her break (the staff used to take turns during breaks from Mabel's room), Lily dropped off into sleep and had a dream; Jane was in Mabel's room with them. She was down on the floor and could not get up but was trying to kick Lily with one leg. Lily said to her, 'What are you trying to do? I rebuke you in Jesus' name'. She then stopped and started to grin at Lily. Then the scenario changed; Jane was lying on top of her daughter in the bed and was trying to pin her down. Lily called on Mabel to get up, and helped her out. Lily then warned Jane that she would be destroyed if she did not stop her wickedness. Lily understood the dream straightaway when she woke up. She was in for an encounter with Jane. However, she knew it was not her whom Jane was confronting but the Lord. So she just committed her into God's hands.

In September of the following year Mabel's dad and mum went on a two weeks holiday. The company management were very impressed with the staff, commenting that the parents could trust them so much to leave their daughter in their care and went on a holiday; something they have not done for years. Mabel was like a new person in the parents' absence, she really thrived, was alert, enjoyed her care and the staff enjoyed caring for her. It was the best time of her life. Sadly, it was not for long. On the night the parents returned from their holiday, she was in distress; moaning and groaning that night. The following morning, she had blood in her urine, then puss and the smell was very offensive. Every sample sent for analysis came back with a result negative of infection. Doctors refused to prescribe antibiotics because of the negative results. Eventually the issue resolved because Lily was praying quietly in the background. The Holy Spirit led Lily to pray for Mabel's relationship with this evil mother to be severed, and the Lord answered the prayer. Mabel began to warm towards the staff more than to the mother and the family. Jane became more and more angry, abusive and racist towards staffs.

Interestingly, she did this when Lily was not there. In Lily's presence, she pretended to be nice.

One night, on the 13th of November, she came while Lily was on duty with her usual intention to manipulate Lily. Lily looked her straight in the eye and told her, 'God loves you but he does not like what you are doing. It is time for you to repent'. She was shocked with the confrontation, made excuses with the cross on her neck and left. Once she said to Lily, 'Your team has taken my daughter away from me'. Lily responded, 'How? We are only helping you by looking after her, and I think we have done a good job and you should appreciate it'. She declined from making any more comment. Earlier on, Lily used to be angry with her because of her wickedness but the Lord taught Lily to direct her anger at the enemy behind her. Lily learnt rather to send her love from her heart. Jane then became relaxed with Lily and not abusive as she was with other staff. However, she was still very manipulative. Being aware of this tendency in her helped Lily each time to deflate the unpleasant situations Jane tried to create most times whenever she was around. She was also attacking Lily spiritually because within this November, Lily had been feeling ill prior to, or at work. Prayer kept Lily on the side of victory every time.

Lily's Church in this season was a praying Church. They used to have an all prayer night at the end of every month, and a 40 days fasting and prayer once a year. These intense prayer times sustained Lily in these encounters with the spirit of wickedness. Lily's Pastor was a great Teacher. His teachings gave Lily great Spiritual insight into most issues in this work and the subsequent attacks on her and her family. The

Pastor and his wife kept counselling and supporting her and her family. Lily also had prayer support from some of the ladies in the Church. Sometimes these ladies just spoke into her life or share revelations with her. It was a very wild season spiritually.

It was also in this month that a friend invited Lily to a prophetic conference at another Church in the neighbouring borough. The presence of the Lord in this conference through the worship, ministry of the Pastor and other speakers released the breaker anointing that further enhanced both Lily's spiritual and physical strength. God used this additional support to equip and strengthened her for this warfare.

Conferences actually became a place for rest, recovery, inspiration and renewed strength. Lily fell in love with a Christian Media Television Channel that used to broadcast conferences from different part of the world frequently. Lily fed on the conferences whenever she was free. She also physically attended some of these conferences. These conferences became her holiday breaks. God used these holidays to give her respite, renew and restore her physical strength and fill her more with His Spirit and lifted her to another level of anointing. Whenever she returned to work after these holidays, Jane could not stand her. She used to literally avoid Lily.

On the 6th of December into the second year of this employment, Mabel was admitted into Hospital because she had become more ill and was having increased seizures. On the 15th of same month, she was diagnosed with brain tumour. The consultant sent her home to die. This was very sad.

On the 18th of same month, Lily was called to come into work early because the day staff were having a difficult time with the family; even dad was becoming aggressive shouting and swearing at the staff. On one hand one could relate this to grief. Lily expressed her understanding as she took over from the day staff. Eventually the family left. Lily and the carer prepared Mabel and put her in bed. They resumed constant watch over her, alternating with each other. At about 11 pm, Lily became ill. She knew instantly this was an attack on her. So she started pleading the Blood of Jesus on herself and in the house, decreed healing scriptures that flooded into her mind. She chose to have the first break where she engaged more in prayers. She felt better thereafter. Mum did not call the whole night, this very unusual. They could not attack Lily physically as they did to the day staff, so they resorted to spiritual attack but again God protected Lily. Attacks on Mabel continued every night, she would be in distress and moaning. Lily just laid hands on her and released peace into her and then she settled.

The night of 26th December was glorious. Lily arrived on duty to see the whole family fussing around Mabel while she was in bed. The atmosphere was chaotic and confusing. Mabel was in obvious distress. The day staff reported that has been the situation all day. Lily was listening to one of her Pastor's messages on the 'Oncoming Wealth Transfer' on her way to work via her car CD player. In this message, the Pastor encouraged listeners to declare, 'I am too connected to the

Almighty God, so devil, don't mess with me'. These words flooded into Lily's heart as she observed at the chaotic atmosphere before her. Lily held unto these words in her mind. Then she walked towards Mabel, held her hand and just said, 'It is okay Mabel'. A great calm fell. Mabel was at peace. The angelic presence was very surreal. Dad left immediately without even saying goodbye. Mum and sister soon followed and left the premises. The day staff were amazed. They looked at Lily with awe, wondering how she was able to bring such calm into the chaos they had endured all day. Lily just encouraged them to hand over and go home. This was the most amazing demonstration of God's

presence and power with Lily in this venture. Lily did not bother to explain this to the rest of the staff because they did not believe and would not understand.

They continued with their work routines, settled Mabel down and had a peaceful night. Mabel survived through the end of that year into the following year. She did not die on the 18th of December as her grandad on the dad's side of the family, and as the family expected. However, she was very ill and expected to pass on anytime. The carers were repeatedly instructed by the Care Company to keep constant watch over her by day and by night. They did it on a rotation basis. Whenever it was Lily's turn, she felt the Holy Spirit's presence in an awesome way. The Spirit led Lily to pray most times in tongues, read some scriptures and sang amazing grace. Mabel used to sing amazing grace with Lily before she became too ill. Now, she sometimes just smiled or nodded her head.

Lily felt Mabel was being comforted by the Lord Himself.

On the 8th of January of the New Year at 20:50, her mum, dad, uncle and aunty walked into the premises. Mum indicated to the carers to go out of Mabel's room and they did. The family shut the door to her room so the carers could not go in. The staff just waited in the lounge and in the office. The staff could hear the family talking but did not understand what they were saying or doing. After about 20 minutes, the family opened the door, mum came out first. Lily asked if they are okay. She responded, 'Yes, we are just going', and they left. When Lily got into Mabel's room, she noticed they had rearranged the soft toys on her bed and placed a white soft toy in the form of a baby owl at the foot of her bed. This was the second time Lily saw this baby owl toy. Lily wondered why they did these but sensed some spiritual implications.

Suddenly, Lily's Spiritual understanding opened to confirm the perception she had previously. The whole of this family was in witchcraft practice, this has been a generational practice. This mum and daughter were the agents until by God's power their relationship was severed. No wonder mum was so mad with the staff. God has destroyed their plan to enslave the staff employed to physically look after Mabel. How wicked the devil is. Lily also recalled once when Mabel came back from one of the Hospital admissions, mum came to help them settle her. She referred to her daughter as a rich girl. Lily used to wonder why she said that, what made a disabled young woman with no hope of a better life rich. It was much later that Lily understood. Now, Lily just took authority in the name of Jesus and destroyed the works of the enemy. Their shift went through uneventfully.

Psalm 27 stayed with Lily all through this night. Here it is in the New Living Translation (NLT):

1. The Lord is my light and my salvation, so why should I be afraid?

2. The Lord is my fortress, protecting me from danger, so why should I tremble?

3. When evil people come to devour me, when my enemies and foes attack me, they will stumble and fall.

4. Though a mighty army surrounds me, my heart will not be afraid. Even if I am attacked, I will remain confident.

5. The one thing I ask of the Lord, the thing I seek most, is to live in the house of the Lord all the days of my life, delighting in the Lord's perfections and meditating in his Temple.

6. For he will conceal me there when troubles come; he will hide me in his sanctuary. He will place me out of reach on a high rock.

7. Then I will hold my head high above my enemies who surround me. At His sanctuary I will offer sacrifices with shouts of joy, singing and praising the Lord with music.

8. Hear me as I pray, O Lord. Be merciful and answer me!

9. My heart has heard you say, 'Come and talk with me'. And my heart responds, 'Lord, I am coming'.

10. Do not turn your back on me. Do not reject your servant in anger. You have always been my helper. Don't leave me now; don't abandon me, O God of my salvation!

11. Even when my mother and father abandoned me, the Lord hold me close.

12. Teach me how to live, O Lord. Lead me along the right path, for my enemies are waiting for me.

13. Do not let me fall into their hands. For they accuse me of things I've never done; with every breath they threaten me with violence.

14. Yet I am confident I will see the Lord's goodness while I am here in the land of the living.

15. Wait patiently for the Lord. Be brave and courageous. Yes, wait patiently for the Lord.

Mabel's health however continued to deteriorate. By the 15th of January, she was having this twitching of her head to the right side, and she could not swallow her saliva. This was very painful for Lily to watch. It was like she was being strangled. Doctors reviewed and order all treatments and feeds withdrawn. The District Nurse came and set up Anticipatory Medication in a Syringe Driver on the 17th. So all the staff had to do now was care for her as a dying person. On this night, the whole family was there. They were talking about spending the night. Their presence was always noisy and more distressing to this poor girl. Lily prayed for them to go so she could have some peace. At midnight, they all decided to go. Thank God for answering Lily's prayers. Lily now seized the time to minister to her in intercessory prayers. By 3 am, Mabel's head jerked into the correct position, the painful twitching resolved and she slept better.

23rd of January was Lily's final night with Mabel. Mum spent all night with her, this was expected in natural circumstances. Lily sat on one side of Mabel's bed and she sat on the other. Lily was enveloped in immense peace and she knew this was the presence of her Lord. Mum was reading a book about angels and fussing over Mabel occasionally. Lily just patted Mabel on the right arm. She felt Mabel relaxed in response to her. Lily had this weird assurance that she has opened up her heart to the Lord and was ready to cross over. At the end of that night duty,

Lily held Mabel's hand and said to her, 'I hope to see you when next I am on duty but if I do not see you anymore, Rest in Peace'. Lily left with a mixed feeling of sadness and fulfilment that she did not understand.

Five days later, on the 28th of January, Lily received a text message from one of her colleagues that informed her Mabel died that morning at 06:08. Lily was very emotional. Mabel was constantly in her heart since her last shift. Lily got out of bed and went downstairs to pray. In the quietness of her heart, she asked the Lord what this was all about, and if she had let Him down in ministering to this family. In her spirit, she heard, 'Mission is accomplished'. Lily was surprised by this response. She did not think Mabel's death was of any good. She was hoping to nurse her to healing and health, and for the whole family to experience the power of God through this miracle, turn to God and be delivered from the power of witchcraft. Lily felt disappointed at her death. She did not understand and as such could not see God's plan and purpose clearly. She felt heavy in her spirit.

However, God is so good and perfect in his planning and actions. He connected Lily with another Pentecostal church that was prophetic in operation. Lily first attended the Prophetic Conference which was on

November the previous year at a friend's invitation. The atmosphere was empowering. This day, the January conference was going on. Lily decided to go and spent the whole day at this conference. It was a Saturday, so she left her husband to babysit.

The Pastor of this Church was speaking this morning. His prophetic words were what lifted the burdens off Lily's spirit. He declared, *'Someone is passing through a situation here that he is wondering if he has done enough. God wants me to tell you, 'You have done all you could'.*

Lily's burden was lifted after receiving these prophetic words. Stanley brought the children to the evening meeting. The family received prayers with laying on of hands that evening. They went back home with a better feeling than they had when they came to the church.

Lily decided not to attend Mabel's funeral which was on the 7th of February. The level of wickedness in her family was appalling, and Lily could not stand any of the family members. She had seen the wickedness in all of them. Their delight in this wickedness was the hardest for Lily to ignore. The most disgusting of all was that the burial was done in the Church. Lily could not stand the sight of all of them in the Church pretending to be godly. Lily recalled Jane once told her how her father's burial was celebrated in the Church. How humans hide their wickedness in the Church is horrible. Let's not forget, God sees it all.

Lily had a revelation at this time about the spirit of Islam. It is the same witchcraft spirit. This also operates in the families and are ruthless, any deviating member has to die. The only difference is that in Islam, the spiritual nature is hidden from the worshippers and their ruthlessness can be seen physically, whereas in witchcraft, the operation is mostly in the spiritual realm and their ruthlessness is subtle. Most physical illnesses are from witchcraft worship and curses. The danger that staff are exposed to in Homecare in the West is awful. Most of these homes are witchcraft covens, and the witches and wizards here are actively feeding on the staff who work there. That was the case here. Every scratch from Mabel used to supply the mum, Jane with blood from the staff. There was a staff that used to challenge Mabel's mum manipulating and controlling ways. She ended up in a terrible accident during her holidays and could not continue in the work. The Lord's protection kept Lily and her household safe. Prior to working with Mabel and after, Lily had done some agency shifts in these covens at various places in this Country. In some she did not know the wickedness operating there though she had the impression of something not being right but now she had the clarity.

After this, Lily began to have vivid dreams of Jane attacking her. Jane was really raging in the spirit realm. Being in this prophetic Church in this season of her life was very crucial. The weekly outpouring meetings became a life source of strength, encouragement and comfort to Lily in this season. On one of these meetings, the 12th of April, Lily responded to the call for ministry, a lovely lady prayed with her. After praying for a while, this lady began to declare, 'You are more than a conqueror. Yes, you are more than a conqueror'. She made the declaration for several times, looking Lily in the eye and laughing as she made them. Suddenly,

Lily's spirit caught up with the prophetic word and she responded to it.

She went home declaring, 'I am more than a conqueror'. Learning to declare this victory lifted Lily to another level spiritually. There is power in what we say to ourselves.

Lily recaptured her life passage words in Isaiah 49:1 – 3

'Listen to me, all you in distant lands! Pay attention you who are far away! The Lord called me before my birth; from the womb he called me by name. He made my words of judgement as sharp as a sword. He has hidden me in the shadow of his hand. I am a sharp arrow in his quiver.

He said to me, 'You are my servant, Lily, and you will bring me glory' (NLT).

Lily's response to the Lord has been and will always be, 'Yes Lord, I am yours. Be glorified in me'. Lily desired for nothing else in her life except

what God has planned and purposed for her. She came into the West because her husband had a job there and as his wife, she had to be by his side. Now, Lily realised God had a plan for bringing them here. He has been directing their step. Lily just had to relax in God's hand and allow him to do whatever he wants to do with her and her family. So the adventure continues.

What Lily got to understand at the end was that the Lord sent her by means of employment into this witchcraft coven where a young precious girl was used as a human sacrifice by a wicked family. He manifested His presence and power through Lily and destroyed the work of darkness that was operating there. This surely infuriated those who were the evil agents, hence the attack on Lily and her family. However, the Lord's presence is with her, and she does not need to fear.

In a dream, the Lord warned Lily not to accept the new job offer by the Care Company. They had offered the Trained Nursing staff health care assistant roles while the pay remained as of Trained Staff. Sounds like a good offer because the Company was working on getting another contract in which Trained Nurses would be needed. Lily would have accepted the offer if the Lord did not warn her not to. With the Lord's direction, Lily returned to agency work and refocused on developing her Counselling Practice as a private business. Lily continued to worship in her Church then while attending the prophetic Church's outpouring weekly meetings and periodic conferences. The enemy's attack on her was intensified. Lily knew the agents were Jane and her family. Their finances, relationship and children were attacked continuously. The Lord proved Himself strong as their defence, provider and protector.

He directed Lily to start a Saturday Bible study with her family and incorporate Holy Communion into it. When she shared the word with Stanley, he objected to it. Knowing, she had heard from the Lord, Lily ignored Stanley and commenced it. The children were happy to take part in it. It was years later Stanley confessed the Lord first instructed him to do this with his family. When he was not implementing it, the Lord then turned to Lily. Stanley was so blind spiritually, he did not even want to agree with Lily. However, the Lord was merciful to them because Lily responded in obedience to whatever he told her to do. This is the beauty of marriage. When one partner is down and not functioning right in their position and responsibilities, the Lord raises the other partner to step in. It is always temporary though. Once, Lily had this vision of a body running around and doing things without the head. She was scared but the Lord made her aware that was supernatural. He was in control, Lily just had to trust him.

In August that year, the Lord directed them to go to camping conference. They heard about it at the prophetic Church. This was also their first camping experience. It did turned out to be very good for the whole family. It was during one of the meetings that one of the speakers, had a prophetic word that was related to them. It went like this; 'There has been a death that has brought defilement into someone's life and family here. The Lord is cleansing that off you'. Lily knew this was for them and received the prophetic word. Stanley came alive in this conference. He used to wake up early, had a time in prayer and went out for a walk in the camp before the meeting began. They had much peace and strength by the end of the conference.

In August the following year, the Lord provided miraculously for Lily and family to go to Israel on a touring holiday. Stanley was also doing only agency work and their Agency did not have much contract therefore no work for them. But God had laid in Lily's heart that they should go when the media channel announced the tour. Lily had to respond in obedience even when Stanley was again resisting because of their financial situation. She began by paying the initial instalment and God opened the door for work and the rest of their needs were met. Going to Israel brought another breakthrough into their family. Their daughter, Victory, had severe headache before and when they arrived in Israel. She was miserable for days and unable to eat until after her baptism in the Jordan River. The next day after the baptism, Victory felt so good and free, ate and enjoyed her meals and the rest of the trip. Their son was also baptised in the Jordan River. What actually happened was that the children went to a youth conference in July that same year and came home to tell Lily and Stanley they both responded to the alter call and recommitted their lives to the Lord. Victory had done this before. So Lily encouraged them to take the next step by having the baptism when they were in Israel about a month after that. It turned out to be the best experience for both of them. God used this tour to heal, restore and refresh them more as individuals and as a family. Going to Israel was a real home coming to their Spiritual root. The story of Jesus in the Bible came more alive to them as they visited the different places that he walked on, taught and performed miracles. It was a special, awesome experience to them as a family.

Chapter 11

Church Experiences

The Church experiences that are going to be described here is that of the West because it has been phenomenal to Lily. You have already read about her awareness and growth in the first local Church that she attended on her arrival to the land. Lily had a cultural shift through the revelations on the Word, this helped remove all her biases and prejudices in regards to dressings and physical appearances. However, relationally, there was a setback. Majority of attendance were white, the few blacks there found it hard to integrate. Lily became aware of the other side of the Western culture in which the people are extremely reserved. The whites kept to themselves and interacted mostly among themselves. As new people into the Church, Lily became aware it was only the few blacks who visited them, invited them to their homes and helped them to settle. The only white people who related with them this way were not even

Christians. They were the parents of Stanley's employer. To Lily this was very sad. Lily also believes this grief the Holy Spirit as well because the Bible says we are all members of the body of Christ and each of us members of one another;

'The human body has many parts, but the many parts make up one whole body. So it is with the body of Christ. Some of us are Jews, some are Gentiles, some are slaves, and some are free. But we have all been baptized into one body by one Spirit, and we all share the same Spirit.

Yes, the body has many different parts, not just one part. If the foot says, 'I am not part of the body because I am not an eye' would that make it any less a part of the body? If the whole body were an eye, how would you hear? Or if your whole body were an ear, how would you smell anything? But our bodies have many parts, and God has put each part just where He wants it. How strange a body would be if it had only one part! Yes, there are many parts, but only one body. The eye can never say to the hand, 'I don't need you'. The head can't say to the feet, 'I don't need you'. In fact some part of the body that seem weakest and least important are actually the most necessary. And the parts we regard as less honourable are those we clothe with the greatest care. So we carefully protect those parts that should not be seen, while the more honourable parts do not require this special care. So God has put the body together such that extra honour and care are given to those parts that have less dignity. This makes for harmony among the members, so that all the members care for each other. If one part suffers, all the parts suffer with it, and if one is honoured, all the parts are glad. All of you together are Christ's body, and each of you is a part of it'. (1 Corinthians 12:12-27. NLT)

Can you imagine the different members of your body not getting along? This would leave you very dysfunctional. No wonder the Church is so dysfunctional on the earth, not effective as God meant it to be. Jesus prayed for the unity of his body in John 17. Lily believes he is still praying for this and it will happen eventually on this earth.

One day during this season, Lily was watching one of the slave trade movies on the television. She felt an incredible anger rose up within her and said out loud, 'How dare people treat other human beings that bad just because of skin colour?' As this question went out of her mouth, the Lord whispered within her, 'There is slavery that is worse than what you have just seen'. Lily was surprised and ask, 'what could it be Lord?' His response came back clear, 'Sin! And it affects both whites and blacks, in fact all human race'. This revelation from the Lord deflated Lily's anger. She began to see all humans as God's creation and as He sees them. Lily became thankful to God for His divine intervention at this time in her life because the anger that she felt could have propelled her towards racism. Lily understood racism comes out of our experiences, real or unreal. This is the power of what we see, hear and the way we understand and process these information. Media plays a huge part in the condition of our world today. It is sad what most news channels report is crime and then we wonder why there is so much crime in our communities. What we focus on is what will become our reality. Lily learned to check what she hears in the news with the Holy Spirit because God's perspective is always the truth. God created all the people with different colours on this earth and he sees people as beautiful. This earth is his garden. The people are all different flowers with different colours, beauty and scents. He loves all his creation just as they are. That is how humans should see, accept and love each other.

As time went on, one of their Christian sisters, who was very helpful to them began to share her vision with them. She felt the Lord was leading her to start a branch of a Pentecostal Church the Community. As their friend they were just very happy to support her. The Church commenced with help from a bigger one, about 100 plus miles away, that was thriving. At some point, a Pastor was sent from their home Country to take up the work. He was a humble and lovely young man. He resided with Lily and family in their small third bedroom in the Council maisonette. This is the Church with which Lily underwent the 49 days of fasting and prayer in January through into February. The longest fast that Lily had ever underwent, and it was very effective.

Unfortunately, the duration of this Church in this Community was short. Some internal conflict began to develop between the leaders. The lovely young Pastor moved on to another location. The new leader moved the Church to another location too far for Lily and family. They decided to end there with this Church and looked for another one. When Lily reflected on how this Church ended, the Lord reminded her of a dream she had in that season that she did not pay much attention to. In that dream, the members were all in the Church, it was in a Community centre. Someone defecated on the floor in the middle of the Church hall. Whoever did this was not known but the members began to move out to avoid the mess. The Lord then asked Lily, 'Did anyone care to clean up the mess?' Of course not, Lily realised. There was no intercessory prayer to support the Church. The enemy is constantly messing up what God is doing or wants to do. It is only intercessory prayer that cleans up any mess from the enemy and clear the way for God's purposes to manifest and prosper on earth. Lily had to repent because she was not playing her part effectively there.

Lily and family decided to go to another Church that was about two miles from their residence. There was something different about this Church, it was livelier and their children loved the Sunday school. Their presence there was brief because they moved house shortly to another part of the town. Here they decided to explore the local Churches in the Community and found one acceptable to them. They made it their home Church. The worship here was inspiring. The Pastor then ministered with a prophetic edge as well. These attributes made going to this h exciting, refreshing and inspiring.

At this stage in Lily's life, she was mostly in Church on Sundays. She was more involved in an interdenominational ladies prayer meeting that moved from Church to Church and on a weekly basis, mostly Saturdays. The leaders were two lovely ladies with a prophetic edge. Lily was introduced to this group by another lovely lady and a prayer warrior in her previous Church. Lily's Spiritual growth and aspirations were also through the Christian Media on television and the ministries she connected with through these media.

This new local Church was one of the most interesting mixed multitudes of a Church that Lily had ever been in. There were leaders who were very nice on the surface but full of unbelief, misbelief and disbelief in the very God they claimed to worship. They loved fun more than the discipline needed for intimacy with God. Interestingly, majority in this category were men. While the women were involved in organising prayer meetings, the men were more into organising parties, sports and fun times with each other. There were also people here who were deeply spiritual. They have grown in their relationship with the Lord so much that they came into the Church every Sunday to do what He told them to do and say what He told them to say. One of these people was a lovely old lady. One week, Lily had cold and her voice was affected. Lily was unable to communicate all week at home. In Church that Sunday, this lovely lady just came and sat by her side. She then turned to her and said, 'I feel the Lord wants me to pray with you. Do you have anything you want prayers for'? Lily motioned with her hand to her mouth. To her surprise she heard this lady declared, 'Satan, In the name of Jesus I command you to take your hands off this voice. This voice preaches the gospel of Jesus Christ and you cannot take it'. Lily was jolted out of her spiritual slumber as she realised her voice was being attacked by the enemy, it was not just an ordinary cold she was having. Lily appreciated her and took her stand. By the end of the day, her voice was restored.

Lily also had some interesting experiences while in this Church. One Sunday, the new Pastor, who took over from the former ordered the service in a unique way. He asked people to raise up their voices in individual worship while the worship team were silent. Suddenly, Lily felt the Holy Spirit whispered in her,' Are you going to be shy now?' Lily felt gently challenged and open up her mouth to offer praise. To her surprise, she found herself praising in tongues. Lily had no clue what she was praying and could not stop myself. The flow eventually stopped as it began. Most of the people's eyes were on her and she felt really embarrassed. Lily had no problem praying in tongues in her prayer times at home. But in this Church, it was a complete strange thing to do. At the end of the service, a gentleman who was sitting on her right hand side turned and said to her, 'Oh is that how you are?' Lily did not know how to respond to his question, and just stared at him. Then he added,

'Anyway, your husband is your biggest challenge'. Lily laughed at this and jokingly said to him, 'Is your wife your biggest challenge?' He looked down as he responded, 'No she has been dead for some years now'. Lily sympathised with him and their conversation ended. As Lily reflected on this conversation on her way home, she had the awareness that it was an encounter with one of the spiritual people in the West, this one was also religious. Interesting!

After a while, the wife of the new Pastor gave birth to a new baby boy, their third son. She developed some back pain after the delivery. This was somehow related to the birth and she had to undergo different investigations and treatments. These did not resolve the problem though. Then one Sunday, both the Pastor and wife were not in Church. One of the elders announced that the Pastor had to take the wife to a hospital appointment as the back pain has become debilitating. Lily found herself angry in the spirit. Before the service was over, they came back and the Pastor came into the Church. Lily went to him and ask if it was possible for her to go and see the wife. The Pastor obliged and asked one of the church workers to escort her. They lived just by the Church. When Lily saw this new mum in pain, the anger in her rose up again. Lily asked if she could pray for her and she gave her consent. Laying her hands on her, Lily rebuked the enemy for touching the Lord's anointed and commanded him to take his dirty hands off her. She was surprised at Lily's prayers but it also woke her up spiritually. They became aware it was not just a post-birth related back pain but the enemy was at work. They took their stand as well and next Sunday, they were in Church, mum and baby healthy and happy. Lily and family did enjoy this Church and went on to make many friends. They introduced one of their neighbours who did not belief to it and they allowed children to go to the children programmes.

Their subsequent move was to a different borough. Again they began to explore the local Churches and found a branch of another Pentecostal Church conducive and joined it. They always wanted to worship with the local Church because it offered them the chance to feel and relate with the Community where they were planted. Majority of members in this Church were black including the Pastor and his wife. The Pastor was a great teacher and a very sensitive and caring person. His teachings sustained Lily through the time she worked with Mabel. It gave Lily most insights and revelations through the Word. The worship was boisterous. They loved everything about this Church and immediately settled in. After a while, Stanley began to miss the previous Church and decided to go back there. At first he was happy to go by himself but after a while decided to demand they all go back. When Lily shared this predicament with the Pastor, he just responded, 'Please do as your husband wants'.

Lily was contemplating going back with Stanley just so that she could keep the peace in the home. She had in mind to continue with the prayer meetings in this new Church. Actually, one of her friends suggested this. Lily was just thinking of it one day when she heard the Lord's voice clearly in her spirit, 'Who told you?' Lily could not respond. The Lord went on, 'Do you both work in the same place?' Lily responded, 'No'. Lily was just working as an agency nurse then while Stanley was still in employment with the local Hospital. And the Lord continued, 'Do you bring the money from your different place of work to care for the family?' Lily responded, 'Yes'. The Lord said, 'Then stay where I want you to'. This was when Lily realised this new local Church was God's choice for them in this season.

Lily then had to tell Stanley, 'Sorry, you are my husband but Jesus is my Lord and I am bound to obey Him'. Lily continued with the local Church with Victory who was happy to be there. They loved it. Her son began to miss his daddy at some point and eventually had to go with him. That's how their home was divided on Sundays in this season, the men to one church and the ladies to another. It was not for too long though. The enemy was actually up to something that God in His awesome wisdom stepped up to interrupt. Prayer at this local Church was intense.

Lily used to find herself feeling like she was giving birth during these prayer times. She knew they needed this prayer support in this season. Eventually, the enemy's hold on Stanley was broken. He began to see clearly and pulled out of the previous Church willingly. They became reunited as a family in one Church, and really got to enjoy the Community.

Being in this Church was also like a season for their children to be connected to their root because prior to this, they were raised mostly in the white community. Lily remembered her daughter saying to her one day; 'I do not understand these people mum, I look like them but I do not talk like them'. Obviously the black community's foreign accent was stronger and more direct than what Victory knew and was used to among her white friends. So Lily had to educate her children about who they are, the culture they have grown up in and how to navigate both cultures and integrate. Lily felt this was a necessary learning for them in this season.

This Church organizes numerous outreaches to impact the Community. Lily's highlight was in one of this Community events. It was a funfair in the local park with other Churches in the Community to bless the Community over the weekend of 12th to 14th of August. The Lord directed Lily to work with one of the white ladies in the Church. She organized prayers in a creative way. That very Saturday morning, Stanley was also organizing a prayer tent with other members of the Church. These were all set up before Lily arrived at the park. Lily had to apologize to Stanley who had expected her to work with him and joined this lady who was outside the tent and in the open field. That was where Lily met one of her neighbours, an old man of 80 years plus. He was walking with a stick and appeared to be in pain. Lily went to say hello to him and then asked what was going on with him. He told Lily he had arthritis on both knees and that the Doctors would not operate on him as they feared he would not recover from the surgical anesthesia. Lily felt a deep compassion rose up in her as she listened to him. When he finished his story, Lily heard herself asking him, 'Do you want to be heal?' He responded, 'This my neighbour has been praying for me'. Lily looked him direct in the eye and ask the question the second time. He responded with a yes. Lily knelt before him, laid her hands on both of his knees and just prayed simply, 'Lord Jesus, would you please show this man how much you love him'. She then commanded his knees to be healed. Lily left him after the prayers and carry on, and he wondered off with his walking stick. But after walking a few metres, he was completely healed and pain free. The next Sunday, he came to Church saying he came to see Lily. He called her the 'praying woman'. Lily told him it is all about Jesus' love for him and directed him to go and tell the Pastor his testimony. Lily refused to talk about this miracle herself because she had been quite aware Jesus never talked about the miracles he did. In some instances, he even told the persons who have received the miracles not to tell anybody. How humble our Lord is. Lily feels she is called to walk in his footstep.

Their season in Church lasted till for over five years. Their transition to the next phase of their Church life for the first time was smooth. The pastor understood their reason for the move, prayed with and released them. He was a Godly and humble man.

Their transition to the next Church was a gradual one First they were invited to a conference by a friend at the end of one year. At the beginning of the subsequent year, they went back for another conference. They loved the conferences. Then they began to attend the weekly outpouring meetings. The worship in this Church hosted the presence of the Lord in an attractive and refreshing way. There was a kind of spiritual satisfaction by just being in this gathering. The prophetic words declared by the Pastor and the team were always encouraging and at times a confirmation of what the Lord has already revealed to Lily.

They were joggling two Churches for about four months during this season. God began to do some deep healing work in Lily through the prayer ministry in this prophetic Church. The first was in one of the weekly outpouring meeting. Another lovely lady declared over her as she stood in the line to receive prayers, 'God will heal your heart'. 'Really! Do I still have any wound in my heart?' Lily thought. By this time, she had walked through a lot of issues in counselling trainings and personal therapy but the list seems to be unending. Anyway, Lily did not know what else to expect. She had no awareness of any current issue.

Some weeks after she had this prophetic word, there was a youth event organized by another lovely lady in the Church. Lily's children wanted to attend this event and Lily had to take them down for it. The lady who prophesied over her was at the reception doing the registration for the Church's weekend event. She asked to register Lily for the event but Lily said to her, 'I do not think I can attend because it is mainly for the members of the Church and I am not one'. This lady responded, 'Oh you have been here long enough'. With that she registered Lily for the event.

Attending this event was life changing for Lily. A lovely couple, taught and ministered to the attendees. Lily's insight came when the wife ministered. She just said after teaching on forgiveness, 'Now close your eyes and ask the Holy Spirit if there is anyone you need to forgive'. As soon as Lily did that, her mother focused. Lily quickly opened her eyes and thought, 'No, it can't be my mother. I have nothing to forgive her for. She was a struggling woman doing what she could for us. I only have to be grateful for her sacrifices'. Lily refused to proceed with the rest of the activities thinking there must be some unholy manipulation going on here.

Two days after that, Lily sent Victory a text message to do something and she did something completely opposite what Lily said. Victory was 15 years old then. Lily was angry with her for the silly mistake. In the middle of her anger, the Holy Spirit whispered into her heart, 'This is why you need to forgive your mother'. 'What?' Lily responded. The Lord went on, 'Because when you were that age, you would have done better. You grew up too quick and you had no childhood. Your daughter is still a child'. Tears ran down Lily's face at this revelation. She had to park her car by the road side as she could not control herself and had a good heart wrenching cry. Deep peace flooded her soul at the end of this cry. Lily became aware this was the heart healing that she needed. She was thankful to the Lord for it.

Lily apologized to her daughter after that and really began to see her just as she is. No more expectation for her daughter to be like she was at her age. There is no way Victory could meet up with how Lily was at that age. Victory had not been exposed to the struggles Lily experienced at her young age. Lily was indeed an adult at that age because of her difficult childhood. She was well able to manage her life and even organized the family due to the difficult situation she grew up in. The downside to that was that Lily never knew how to relax and play as a child. She was always thinking, planning and working, always on the go. This was also the first time Lily became aware of the deep healing forgiveness can release into someone's life. It was amazing, and Lily was excited to let others know about it.

They could have continued joggling two Churches but their children fell more in love with the Prophetic Church. They began to attend the youth meetings and really got to enjoy the gatherings. From there, they were invited to the Sunday school. At their request, Lily decided to take them. As a mum, she just wanted her children to enjoy their lives including going to the Church. They got to love the youth meetings on Sundays as well. It got to the point they would ask Lily and Stanley on Saturday evenings which Church they are going to on Sunday. If the parents said the local Church, they did not want to get out of bed in the morning, but if they said the prophetic Church, the children would be ready for Church the next day before them. Eventually, Lily and Stanley had to make a difficult decision. They decided Lily continue to take the children on Sundays to the prophetic Church while Stanley stays at the local Church. This family division did not go down well with the local Church because they were part of the leadership team. After some reflections, they realised God was using the children to lead them this time around and accepted to move on.

Lily decided to do the training organised by the Prophetic Church the year the joined the Church fully. She felt she needed to move into another level in her relationship with God. Some conflict was still going on in their home disrupting their family life and relationship constantly. Part of this was attacks from the enemy and Lily felt she needed to be empowered so she could help herself and her family. As a family they have struggled most times but in this season, the struggle had escalated. Victory was struggling emotionally and mentally, their son's health was constantly failing, Stanley did not know what to do because he did not really dealt with his issues and so resorted to being angry most times. This created a lot of conflict in their relationship because most times Lily tried to protect the children from his anger and he did not like it. The problem was as an adult, Lily expected Stanley to take responsibility for his feelings and thoughts. The children being helpless needed protection. In it all their lives was being stressed with financial challenges because Stanley was not doing regular shifts.

It was like living in a whirl wind continuously with occasional short breaks and relief. The training turned out to be exceptional and just what Lily needed for the season. The co-ordinator of the training opened the first session on the 26th of February with a word God told him; 'You need wisdom to apply love'. He went on to expound on love as a curtain rail using Mathew 22:37-40;

Jesus replied, 'You must love the Lord your God with all your heart, all your soul, and all your mind. This is the first and greatest commandment.

A second is equally important: 'love your neighbour as yourself'. The entire law and all the demands of the prophets are based on these two commandments' (NLT)

Lily's insight to this scripture was that to walk in love, we have to first accept God's love through Jesus Christ, chose to respond to God's love with all of our heart, soul and mind. This is when we can have healthy love for ourselves and for others.

Maturity in love is about seeing others as God sees them and allowing God's love to flow through us to them. This love is supernatural because it comes from our heavenly Father who is love. God's love is firm, limitless, and selfless and does not depend on how others respond, and of course full of wisdom. Lily realized she is still a work in progress where this love is concerned. She needed wisdom on how to love Stanley, loving him was her biggest challenge. Lily earnestly sought the Lord for this. She wanted the cycle of conflict in their home to end and if it all depended on her, so be it.

God took Lily up for it and used this season to help her deal with deep heart issues that she was not aware of. Part of the training was engaging in the daily devotionals that they were given. One day, Lily had to read Psalm 139:

O Lord, you have examined my heart and know everything about me. You know when I sit down or stand up. You know my thoughts even when I'm far away. You see me when I travel and when I rest at home. You know everything I do. You know what I am going to say before I say it, Lord. You go before me and follow me. You place your hand of blessing on my head. Such knowledge is too wonderful for me, too great for me to understand! I can never escape from your Spirit! I can never get away from your presence! If I go up to heaven, you are there; if I go down to the grave, you are there. If I ride the wings of the morning, if I dwell by the farthest oceans, even there your hand will guide me and your strength will support me. If I could ask the darkness to hide me and the light around me to become night-but even in darkness I cannot hide from you. To you the night shines as bright as day. Darkness and light are the same to you. You made all the delicate, inner parts of my body and knit me together in my mother's womb. Thank you for making me so wonderfully complex! Your workmanship is marvellous-how well I know it. You watched me as I was being formed in utter seclusion, as I was woven together in the dark of the womb. You saw me before I was born. Every day of my life was recorded in your book. Every moment was laid out before a single had passed. How precious are your thoughts about me, O God? They cannot be numbered! I can't even count them; they outnumber the grains of sand! And when I wake up, you are still with me!

O God, if only you would destroy the wicked! Get out of my life, you murderers! They blaspheme you; your enemies misuse your name. O

Lord, shouldn't I hate those who hate you? Shouldn't I despise those who oppose you? Yes, I hate them with total hatred, for your enemies are my enemies.

Search me, O God, and know my heart; test me and know my anxious thoughts. Point out anything in me that offends you, and lead me along the path of everlasting life (NLT).

Impressed by how David opened up his heart to the Lord in this Psalm. Lily felt the need to do same at the end, the last part of it leaped into her heart so she closed her eyes and asks the Holy Spirit, 'Lord is there anything in me that offends you?' Lily had an immediate response that surprised her, 'Pride'. Lily was shocked because she never saw herself as a proud person. Then she remember God is always right. She repented and then asked God to show her the prideful actions and attitudes because she needed to have the self-awareness. This would enable her to guard against it. God made her aware that how Lily actually saw herself as a shy person was pride. Lily was more surprised but the Lord went on to help her understand how this was pride. There were a couple of times she felt the Lord's leading to talk to someone but retreated because this person was a prominent figure in the Church and the word was a kind of reprimanding. The Lord made her realise she was thinking more about herself in those instances rather than focusing on him and obeying him. Suddenly Lily's definition of pride changed. It was not about puffing up but more of thinking excessively of one's own self to the extent that acting out of one's comfort zone is impeded. To overcome this pride, Lily needed to learn to walk in boldness and be authentic in her relationships. Thank God the Holy Spirit was her helper. Lily just needed to submit to him daily and be sensitive to his leading. It was very easy to fall back into her default self but every time this happened, the Holy Spirit was there to convict her and help her step out with boldness again. It became a daily walk for her.

The students also read and reviewed some books during the course. The book that made a lasting impact on Lily and in her relationship was by Jack Frost; 'From Spiritual Slavery to Spiritual Son-ship. Your Destiny Awaits You'. Jack Frost's description of his restless, unstable and adventurous life was just like Stanley's. When Lily finished reading the book, she thought, 'How I wish his wife had written about her own experiences and how she coped so I could learn from her'. Then the Lord responded in her heart, 'Do you think if the wife had known all about him as you do about your husband and refuse to submit to him, they would have come into their destiny?' This response also surprised Lily because up till then, she did not know she was refusing to submit to her husband. Again, she repented and then went to Stanley and asked how he wants her to support him. He said he wanted Lily to come out with him to do evangelism. Up to this time he was doing it by himself, he never asked Lily to go out with him and Lily did not bother because he was always into one thing or another. He was starting projects and stopping as he wanted, and at times not even discussing issues with Lily.

Lily just felt he was doing his own thing while she focused on her work, studies and housekeeping.

On the 25th of April that year, Lily went out with Stanley for the first time for the evangelism in their Town Centre. The Holy Spirit led them first into the Council House and quickened them to decree Joshua 1:3 over the Community.

'I promise you what I promise Moses: Wherever you set your foot, you will be on land I have given you' (Joshua 1:3 NLT)

People responded to the gospel, accepted the tracts and some just had questions that they needed answers for. The Holy Spirit's presence was very tangible. They began to go out on a weekly basis after this. Here's some of the testimonies from their weekly evangelism adventure: on the afternoon of 11th of July at this Town Centre, a man came to them, at first he was talking with Stanley. Lily was giving out tracts to some of the people passing by when she felt a notch in her spirit to stop and listen to this man. He was mainly blaming others for not living right. Lily started to pray silently for the Holy Spirit to intervene. He then mentioned his wife was poorly. Lily seized the chance and asked what the sickness was and he said it was kidney failure. Lily went on to tell him God could heal his wife. Stanley joined to encourage him to focus on his need rather than blaming others. With his consent, they ended up praying for his wife's healing and leading him in a prayer of repentance and rededication of his life to God. Prior to this, he was quoting lots of scriptures to Lily and Stanley saying he knew about God from his grandmother. His facial expression changed after the prayers, he was more at peace. He confessed he did not want to go to them initially but eventually did and it was nice talking to them. Lily and Stanley realised the Holy Spirit drew him to them because God wanted to bless him. And that became their regular experiences every time that they went out. God would just draw the people who were hungry or in need of him to them, and thereby met their needs. This man that they prayed for later reported his wife healed and his whole family accepted the Lord into their lives. It was wonderful.

Another thing the Lord opened Lily's awareness to, was that He had a destiny for them. Lily felt they were walking in this destiny by reaching out to souls for Him. They also began to minister to people together in their home in the form of Pastoral care. On one occasion, Lily had completed sessions of counselling with the wife but could not do the same with the husband though he had issues with depression and anger. The man was not willing to go to another counsellor either. It was the wife who first came to Lily for counselling. Lily could not counsel the husband thereafter to avoid breaching professional standard. So she arranged to work with him in a pastoral way and with Stanley. They listened to and led him in prayers of repentance, forgiveness and reestablishing his relationship with God. God was faithful in releasing healing and freedom into this man's life. It was amazing to see him hearing from God again and journaling what God was saying to him. He left their home smiling and thankful.

By the time Lily completed the training her life was greatly transformed. Her heart was healed and her mind was more renewed. Lily found herself walking in more spiritual authority and power. For instance whenever she went to nursing work in any of the hospitals and there was chaos, disruptions and the subsequent stress on the staff, Lily just said, 'It will be alright now'. Calm and order was the norm during the shift. The staff were thankful at the end and the patients would say, 'It has been the only night I ever slept during my admission here'. Lily was quite aware of increased demonic activities in the Hospital wards and took authority over them whenever she entered any Ward to work in.

Most times some patients opened up and asked Lily questions that led to her telling them about God's love for them. The Hospital Wards are the most unsafe places to be or work in without the power of God. But Lily had lots of fun whenever she was there. It was just one of the adventures living with God. Lily also began to walk in a prophetic anointing. One day, she felt like and went for a walk in her neighbourhood in a street she had never walked through. This street was just behind hers. As Lily passed by a house with some unusual moulded images in the front garden, she heard in her spirit, 'This is the stronghold in this Community. Decree that it be pulled down'. Sensing this was the Lord, Lily just made the decree, 'Strong hold be pulled down in Jesus name', and carried on with her walk. A few days after, a neighbour who was living in this street, they had a shared fence, suddenly said to Lily from over the fence, 'I have been planning to cut this tree down but every time I become ill and unable to do it'. This was a huge and tall tree on his side of the garden and at the boundary between them. Every time it was windy, they always look at that tree and pray it would not fall because it would do a lot of damage to the surrounding houses. So when this man said that Lily just responded, 'Next time when you plan, you will certainly do it'. A few days later, he cut down the tree with the help of the tree experts. Amazing!

Lily's transformation inspired Stanley and he decided to attend the next training the following year. His experience at the end helped him to address a lot of the issues in his life that he was not aware off and also in his relationship with others. Stanley is a lovely, kind, faithful and generous man, but he also had a difficult childhood that left him with some emotional wounds and pains that he was not aware of. To cope with life he had developed some very strong self-defensive ways which were mostly pride and anger. This made relating with him difficult. His strong self-independence made it even difficult for him to learn to depend on God or submit to authority figures that God placed over him at times. He tends to do most things with a lot of self-effort, had very high expectations and then crash with disappointment when things did not turned out the way he had expected. He was always excited in starting new projects but gave up easily when he met with resistance and challenges. Lily found it even difficult helping him at times as he did not value or accept whatever she said. Lily finally resorted to only pray for him and trusting God to help him. However, this training did helped both Lily and Stanley to become aware of and dealt with most of their heart issues. They were faced with the daily challenges and choices of living out their freedom.

For Lily, her life and the challenges became daily adventures with the Lord. Lily had the conviction that everything that happened or will ever happen in her life was meant to happen, and God is not surprised by any of these events. Trusting God with her life and learning to talk to Him about everything she encountered in this life was the only sure way to navigate through life challenges. Once Lily reacted to Stanley's anger by being angry with him. In the heat of this argument, she heard in her inside 'Come into my presence'. She knew this was the Lord but she responded, 'No Lord, I'm just too angry'. The Word came again and by the third time, Lily stopped confronting her husband. She just left him and went upstairs into their bedroom and open up to the Lord by releasing all her anger, frustration and tears before the Lord. His presence was awesome. Lily felt His loving arms wrapped around her, His peace filled her soul, and all the storm within and around her was calm. Stanley also felt him. When Lily went downstairs after that, Stanley apologised. Lily forgave him, they prayed and their relationship was restored. Marital relationship is very challenging but they have been able to make it and stay married with God's help.

The encouragement to the reader here is to develop his or her relationship with God because he understands you more than anyone else. You can trust God with your most scary emotions and thoughts.

He wants to be your friend. Just let Him!

Reflect on the words of this old time song:

What a friend we have in Jesus

All our sins and grief to bear

What a privilege to carry

Everything to God in prayer

Yes, we can carry everything to God. Prayer is a special privilege when we open up our hearts to the Lord in a sincere way, listen to His response in our inner being or through his Words in the Bible and respond to Him in obedience. God is not interested in our eloquence as some religion teaches. He just wants us to be ourselves with Him as we can be with our best and trusted friend. This is the freedom that Jesus came to give us. There is freedom in relating with God as our Father and as our Friend. And He is a very loving and caring Father. He understands us more than anyone else. He can be trusted.

It is important for us as God's children to learn to follow the leading of His Spirit. He wants to lead us daily and provide us with all that we need. He wants to help us overcome the strategies of the enemy and live in daily victory. Obedience to God is the key to a successful and prosperous life.

Deuteronomy 11:27,

'You will be blessed if you obey the commands of the Lord your God....'

Lily became aware God moved them through the different Churches in order to protect them and help them escape the traps of the enemy. It was all for their good. God always want to lead His children into victory in every area of their lives. All that they had to do was listen to and follow His leadership. He knows the way and has their future all planned out.

Conclusion

In concluding this book, let's reflect on this scripture in Jeremiah 18: 1 - 6

'The Lord gave another message to Jeremiah, He said, 'go down to the potter's shop and I will speak to you there' So I did as he told me and found the potter working at his wheel. But the jar he was making did not turn out as he had hoped, so he crushed it into a lump of clay again and started over. Then the Lord gave me this message: O Israel, can I not do to you as this potter has done to this clay. As the clay is in the potter's hand, so are you in my hand'.

God created us perfect. He is the potter while we are the clay. He sees us beautiful as His creation. And He has a good plan for each and every one of us as stated in Jeremiah 29:11;

'For I know the plans I have for you', 'says the Lord'. They are plans for good and not for disaster, to give you a future and a hope.

However, in the course of birth, growth and surrounding situations and environments, something goes wrong and we become marred but God never let go of us. He does not throw us away no matter how marred we have become. Unlike the clay which does not resist the potter, our choices and responses to life challenges contributes to our pain as we tend to resist God. But God is so patient that He will wait on us until such a time that we become aware of His love for us, open up our heart to receive this love. The process of breaking up and remoulding then begins but at the pace that we yield in His hand. To some of us, the transformation will be quicker than in others. It all depends on how our hearts have become harden through the traumas of life and how willing we are able to open up to Him. In this process, God's aim is to heal, restore and make us whole; bringing us to the place of His original intent for us so we can live the abundant life He planned for us to live. This is where we experience His peace, love and joy; the Kingdom life.

Romans 14:17;

'For the Kingdom of God is not a matter of what we eat or drink, but living a life of goodness and peace and joy in the Holy Spirit'

The final encouragement to the reader is to seek to live the Kingdom life in every area of your life. This is the life our heavenly Father wants us to live. And this is the life that glorifies him on this earth by drawing others to Him.

My prayer and hope is that God will use the story in this book to bless individuals, families and nations by opening their spiritual understanding to know **The Only True God and Jesus Christ of Nazareth, His Son as the Only Way to this God.**

This will turn people away from darkness to **The Light** as they open their hearts to His love, mercy and grace. God will free them from the power of sin and the devil and established His Kingdom in their lives, families and nations.

So be blessed exceedingly abundantly as you read this book!

God loves you beyond your wildest imagination!

Believe His love!

Receive His love!!

Be empowered by His love!!!

And enjoy your adventure with the living God!!!!!!!

Reflect on this scripture:

'Keep me safe, O God, for I have come to you for refuge.

I said to the Lord, 'You are my master! Every good thing I have comes from you'.

The godly people in the land are my true heroes! I take pleasure in them!

Troubles multiply for those who chase after other gods, I will not take part in their sacrifices of blood or even speak the names of their god.

Lord you alone are my inheritance, my cup of blessing. You guard all that is mine.

The land you have given me is a pleasant land. What a wonderful inheritance!

I will bless the Lord who guides me; even at night my heart instructs me

I know the Lord is always with me. I will not be shaken, for he is right beside me.

No wonder my heart is glad, and I rejoice. My body rests in safety.

For you will not leave my soul among the dead, or allow your holy one to rot in the grave.

You will show me the way of life, granting me the joy of your presence and the pleasures of living with you forever' (Psalm 16).

Yes, you can have the pleasure of living with God while here on this earth and in eternity after this life. If you do not have this relationship with God, you can have it right now if you want. Just pray this prayer:

Father God, thank you for loving me so much that you sent Jesus to die for my sins.

Jesus, thank for taking my place; bearing my sin on your body and nailing them to the cross and setting me free from them.

Today, I chose to repent from all the wrong things that I have done, the good things that I have not done, the sins, wickedness, iniquity and transgressions that I have inherited from my previous generations (stop and mention the sins that you are aware of). I am very sorry for these sins. Please Lord forgive me. Wash and cleanse me with your precious Blood.

Today also, I chose to forgive everyone who have wronged or offended me in anyway (now stop and mention those that come into your mind and declare you forgive them out loud).

Lord Jesus, I chose you as my Lord and Saviour today. Please fill me with your Spirit and make me a child of God. Thank you, Lord.

If you have prayed this sincerely in your heart, believe he has heard you and you are save.

'Congratulations and welcome to the family of God'.

The next thing you need to do is start to study your Bible daily, start with the New Testament, that is, from the Gospel of Mathew down to Revelation. You can study the Old Testament after this. The reason why this recommendation is made here is because you need to develop your relationship with Jesus and The Holy Spirit by learning to hear from and see him in the written word as the Living Word. Once you are able to hear his voice and follow him in obedience the rest will be easy. Ask him to lead you to the right Church family where you will be able to develop and grow as you fellowship with others. He will help you make the right decisions and choices as you navigate life. And you will have your own unique adventure with him.

Again, welcome to God's family. May he bless and keep you by the power of his love!

Notes / Reflection

Well done for reading this book to the end. Now, I want to encourage you to reflect on what you have read. You can use the following headings or do it your own way:

- *What have you become aware of about God by reading this book?*

- *What have you become aware of about yourself?*

- *What would you change about your life now?*

- *What difference would this change make to your life and relationships?*

Bible Credits

Unless otherwise noted, most Scripture quotations are taken from the NLT (New Living Translation).

Other versions recommended are:

King James Version (KJV).

The Amplified Bible.

The Passion Translation.

The Message.

www.ingramcontent.com/pod-product-compliance
Lightning Source LLC
LaVergne TN
LVHW010215070526
838199LV00062B/4594